Also by Steven Key Meyers

Fiction

The Last Posse

Another's Fool

Junkie, Indiana

My Mad Russian: Three Tales

The Wedding on Big Bone Hill

Queer's Progress

New York / Siena: Two Short Novels

All That Money

Good People

Non-Fiction

I Remember Caramoor: A Memoir

*The Man in the Balloon:
Harvey Joiner's Wondrous 1877*

A Journal of the Plague Year,

and Other Plays and Adaptations

Steven Key Meyers

A Journal of the Plague Year, and Other Plays and Adaptations

Copyright © 2019 Steven Key Meyers

ISBN: 978-1-7330465-0-3

Published by Steven Key Meyers/The Smash-and-Grab Press

All rights reserved. No part of this publication may be reproduced, stored in a retrieval system or transmitted in any form or by any means, electronic, mechanical, recording or otherwise, without the prior written permission of the author.

Printed on acid-free paper.

All characters appearing in these works are fictitious. Any resemblance to real persons, living or dead, is coincidental. Queries about performance rights should be directed to the author at stevenkeymeyers@stevenkeymeyers.com.

Cover by Todd Engel.

2019

First Edition

A Journal of the Plague Year,

and Other Plays and Adaptations

Contents

Author's Preface 9

A Journal of the Plague Year 21
Chesterfield to His Son 123
Dr. Knox and Mr. Banner 161

One-Act Plays

The Happy Ending 279
My Gamaliel 291
The Garden Party 315
Seductions of a Wedding Night 341
Chocolate Meringue Pie 373

Author's Preface

I'm a novelist who started out a playwright. When I moved to Manhattan in 1978, I promptly fell in love with theatre, and by the time I moved on in 1994 had seen hundreds of plays, and written all but one of these below. (Naturally, since leaving New York, I've seen only a handful.)

One-Act Plays

In 1989 I celebrated my escapes from academia and from running a family business that had plunged me into depression by assigning myself an apprenticeship writing one-act plays, and for five or six years wrote plays exclusively (well, and a screenplay, derived from Swinburne yet). Having now re-read them for the first time in twenty years, I flatter myself that they remain fresh and original.

My first play was *My Gamaliel*, inspired by the summer I spent in Alaska before going to New York, doing assessment work on mining claims as a geological field assistant (my two-man team established that Red Mountain in the Alaska Range is a zinc massif; one day on its slopes a grizzly bear interrupted me as I lay reading Jane Austen). At the museum in Seward, I saw a display about President Warren G. Harding's visit to the town one morning in 1923, the final stop of his "Journey of Understanding," and learned that the town's mayor had asked his townspeople to show the President respect by staying indoors and out of his way. Harding accordingly wandered the streets by his lonesome, then sailed south. Collapsing on board, he was taken off comatose at San Francisco and died. The obvious question: What happened that morning in Seward?

The Happy Ending (1990) reminds me that in the '80s you could buy a *Daily Worker* on West 23rd Street's sidewalk and chat with the man selling it, his face shining with idealism as he deflected jibes from passersby *("Go back to Russia, ya dirty Red!")*. Lofts in the neighborhood still clacked with Linotype machines, and almost every store—for whatever strange reason—had a stuffed rodent or small mammal mounted in the window.

The Garden Party (1990) takes place backstage at one, while voices off rise high and hilarious on spiked punch. When an old friend wanders into the pantry, the hunter becomes the hunted—the philanderer past his prime finds his kitten victim grown up into a panther. As told in *I Remember Caramoor,* my memoir of being that famous Westchester County estate's teenaged underbutler, my play was inspired by its 1970 garden party, when the daughter of Sir Oswald Birley, who had painted Mrs. Lucie Bigelow Rosen's portrait, visited us in the pantry and became reacquainted with Mr. Clark, the butler. I wrote the play knowing nothing about her except her father's name and what I could observe (including the purple jumpsuit), ignorant until the dawning of the Internet of Maxime de la Falaise's own fame.

In *Seductions of a Wedding Night* (1991) two strangers in Iowa for a wedding share a motel room. One man is gay, the other very young. The younger helps the elder salivate (where's the sport in that?), while the elder pretends not to notice the youth's beauty (where's the justice?), as each entertains the possibilities. It's an energetic little piece.

Chocolate Meringue Pie (1992) was inspired by an incident of my step-grandmother's visit shortly after my grandfather's death (I was nine), when she accidentally locked herself out of the house one morning. Soon she came out of retirement and returned to teaching on the Navajo Indian Reservation. Despite being from Indiana, she was the sweetest person I've ever met.

So at the nadir of its fortunes, I moved to New York City and got a job as proofreader-cum-messenger at a type shop on West 25th Street and an apartment in the far East Village, on the terrifying block of East Tenth Street between Avenues B and C, named by the New York *Daily News* one of the city's worst. For blocks around was nothing but a bombed-out wasteland roamed by junkies, predators, rats and artists, most of the old tenements being abandoned or rubble. Its remote air reminded me of the Rockies above timberline, but it was far more dangerous. I was mugged once with a gun, again with a club, and one night awoke to the touch of an intruder's knife. Strangely enough, my phone number was apparently similar enough to Mark Strand's that I used to field plummy-voiced calls meant for him.

Fortunately in 1981 I moved to a safer neighborhood, Hell's Kitchen—West 54th Street near Ninth Avenue—that was also more convenient to City College and Columbia University, where I earned degrees in English Lit (naturally learning ten times more at CCNY than at Columbia).

Meanwhile AIDS came in and took over. I first heard about an unknown disease killing a handful of gay men in hospitals across Manhattan from a medical-resident friend in the summer of 1980, a year before the famous New York *Times* article of July 3, 1981. But soon enough that distant drumbeat of doom was banging away right in front of my face and everybody else's, and indiscriminately taking friends, lovers, enemies, acquaintances, friends of friends, colleagues and teachers.

A Journal of the Plague Year

Adapting Daniel Defoe's *A Journal of the Plague Year* for the stage seemed a natural response. I don't know how many read his classic these days (surely a graphic novel of it would sell?), but it's a terrific book, throbbing with life however saturated by death. Defoe was a little boy in 1665 when bubonic plague killed a quarter of the people of his London. In 1721, as another epidemic threatened, the old man called on his memory and vivid commercial instincts to write two plague books.

The rarer one, which I luckily stumbled across at the New York Public Library, is *Due Preparations for the Plague*. In dialogue form, it follows the divergent strategies of two families (the play's Tydings and Selkirk families) in the face of the epidemic, replete with windy injunctions to *pray, pray, pray*. At least *Due Preparations* gave Defoe a place to stash the pieties that might otherwise have marred his other plague book, so largely free of them.

AND OTHER PLAYS AND ADAPTATIONS –

That second book, *A Journal of the Plague Year,* purports to be the journal of one "H.F.," a Whitechapel saddler who, seeing the plague sweep into his city, feels compelled to view and record its horrors. He patrols London and returns home to write up his "ordinary memorandums," depending less on prayer to survive than on the practical sanitary precepts of his physician friend Dr. Heath. But it seems that his forays in search of journal material help preserve him, too, almost as if Defoe offers up H.F.'s experience as a paradigm for the writer's life: living always in plague time, able to rely on himself only (shades of *Robinson Crusoe),* surviving so as to make an ultimately honest accounting: "Yet I *alive!"*

Other sources for my adaptation were *Loimologia; or, an Historical Account of the Plague in London in 1665,* by Nathaniel Hodges (ca. 1666), *God's Terrible Voice in the City,* by Thomas Vincent (ca. 1666) and *The Great Plague in London 1665,* by Walter George Bell (1924).

In 1993, The New York Theatre Workshop kindly gave the play a reading, directed by Michael Petshaft, with Darryl Theirse reading Foe and the participation of Rinne Groff, Paul Harris, Roberta Levine, Bruce Katzman, Molly Powell, Brian Keane, Martin Moran and—fresh from snuggling under a blanket with Madonna during breaks in filming her *Bad Girl* video, in which he played a detective—Frank Raiter. The actors were excellent but—entirely owing to my script as it then was—the reading flatter than a pancake. James Nicola, NYTW's Artistic Director, advised me to concentrate on Defoe's hints that the government knew more about the plague than it cared to let on *("There's* your play!"); I disagreed. The reading's great result was that it enabled me to see how to make the script dimensional — how to raise the play up from print to action.

I'm grateful to Charas/El Bohio Community Center — that remarkable institution (now unfortunately defunct) that for more than twenty years squatted in an abandoned schoolhouse between East Ninth and Tenth Streets (on my old block!) — for producing *A Journal of the Plague Year* as an Actors' Equity Showcase in 1994. (And I was delighted to meet there a board member, the fine actor and movie star Luis Guzman.)

We rehearsed in an upstairs classroom during the incomparable month of May, the old school building charged with activity, the neighborhood's very atmosphere electric — so different from when I'd lived there fifteen years earlier. One evening we witnessed a confrontation on Ninth Street between FBI agents and the priest who, to this day, is said to harbor millions from an armored-car heist. In cosmic irony as we rehearsed our play about plague and terror, the World Trade Center was a presiding presence, soaring up seemingly just outside our windows.

Our audiences laughed and cried, making the run a success in every way that counts. The cast was superb. Gino Montesinos played Foe, Katherine Sandberg was Judith; Ben Soto, Heath, with Claudia Arenas (Esther Selkirk), James K. Wuensch (Tydings), Emily Lester (Mrs. Tydings), John E. Slagle (John Selkirk) and Timothy Durkin (Martindale). Russell Hodgson designed and ran the evocative lighting, Sang-Jin Lee designed and sourced the exquisite costumes (Kyung-Ah Kang was Costume Assistant) and John E. Slagle, again, built ingenious and effective sets and props. David Paul composed haunting themes in period dance rhythms, which violinists Karen Hansen and Sara Parkins improvised upon in performance. Stage Manager Kirsten E.C. Haussermann was also, one weekend, an actor's game and capable fill-in, and, with Carrie P. Haussermann (Technical Staff), incomparably deft at helping with the actors' quick changes. Charas's Roberto Badillo, Carlos Baez, Robin Michaels, Ulla Neuerburg, Alexander Perez, Ali Perez, Fabiana Reyez, Richard Velez and Executive Director Carlos Chino Garcia contributed to the production's success. Helpful criticism of the script came from Gary Bird, Anthony Brazile, Peter Brickelbank, Linda Chapman, Bettina Drew, Rob Glasser, Norman Kelvin, Tony Phelan, Bruce Phemister, Frank Rouda, Glen Sparer, Lizabeth Spires, and especially Albert F. Pesant, as well as from my parents, Jean Meyers and Harold Burton Meyers, who, with Sheila Meyers and Terry Meyers, also generously helped underwrite the production. The scheduled director pulling out at the last minute, I directed. The late Armando Perez, Charas's Artistic Director and the play's producer, declared it the best thing Charas ever did.

Chesterfield to His Son

Trust me, reading Lord Chesterfield's letters to his son yields little pleasure; not only are they endless — sprawling across multiple volumes even in abridged editions — and endlessly repetitive, but bottomlessly dull. My late friend Bruce Phemister was subjected, growing up, to Sunday readings from them by his father, the surgeon for whom the University of Chicago named a building, and scarred for life. When I told Bruce that, adapting the letters into a play, I was discovering a human and relatable character, he was hostile. "Who cares?" he said. "So what?"

But buried in what amounts to a written code of civility (remember civility?) is a heartsick father willing to do *anything*—even reveal himself utterly—to help his son make his way in the world. Shrewd, observant, without hypocrisy, he knows that civility is desirable not because it's Christ-like but because it drips like oil into the gearing of the way the world works, giving the benefit of greater smoothness. Looking unblinkingly at how men and women behave, Chesterfield instructs his son in how to conduct himself so as best to promote his interests. Even as fathers go, Chesterfield must have been unbearable, but it's easy to see that he loved his son.

My adaptation interpolates not more than two dozen words of my own; it's Chesterfield's voice as teased out from his *Letters* that transforms that most forbidding and self-conscious of men to an unself-conscious, loving clown. (My ideal casting would be Charlie Chaplin, F. Murray Abraham or Bill Irwin.) For what it's worth, I wrote *Chesterfield to His Son* in Los Angeles in 1995 with one ear cocked to O.J. Simpson's trial (and the jury's inevitable verdict) on the radio.

Dr. Knox and Mr. Banner

Dr. Knox and Mr. Banner (1992) began with my reading in the late '80s an article in *The Advocate,* I forget by whom, that in passing mentioned a 19th-century German scientist whose theory was that same-sex attraction is a trait carried by the blood, thus "curable" by means of transfusion. I never knew (or wanted to know) more than this, but set my play in the slightly more familiar terrain of London.

AND OTHER PLAYS AND ADAPTATIONS –

In the long, painful course of writing my first full-length work, I absorbed a writer's basic lesson thus: One Monday morning I was suffering at my desk, wishing I were any place else on earth, when suddenly I wondered what might be on at the Metropolitan Museum of Art. Reasoning that a brisk walk uptown and two hours' glance inside would well reward me for a day's missed writing, I hurried up, only to discover what I knew very well, that the Met (in those days) was closed on Mondays. I trudged home, my day wasted, except for having learned something useful about a writer's discipline.

Dr. Knox and Mr. Banner's energy delights me. I never before realized how Shavian a play it is — fitting tribute, I hope, to all the glorious Shaw I saw in New York.

It was not any lack of commercial success that caused me to abandon playwriting in favor of writing novels (no more am I discouraged by my novels' commercial failure), but my discovery that fiction better enables my peculiar gift of writing characters out to make sense of the world by telling themselves stories. Early in 1996 I began writing a novel, *Queer's Progress*, whose first draft was an expansive epic in three voices. And that was it; home at last.

But of course the plays, too, feature characters who tell themselves stories: Harry Foe in *Plague Year* impresses narrative over the chaos of his experience and apparently thus saves himself. Knox and Banner construct intricate theories and justifications concerning their relationship, before one accepts his own authenticity at any cost and the other rejects his. Nelma of *My Gamaliel* spins herself a fable in order to redeem Alaska's promise and her marriage. *The Happy Ending*'s Old Agitator nimbly overlays a new narrative, fitter for his present circumstances, over an outdated one. Cynthia, encountering in *The Garden Party* the man who launched *her* story, brings it full circle and makes it big. In rehearsing every possibility from a night's serendipity, Dan in *Seductions of a Wedding Night* comes to a rueful recognition of himself. Similarly, in *Chocolate Meringue Pie* Violet arrives at recognition and acceptance after examining her life through a filter of cherished recipes. Lord Chesterfield, who has all the answers, recites them *ad nauseum* to his son, until released to be a doting grandfather by the one event he never foresaw.

Life is so inchoate, so unpredictable—and always so cheap—it's no wonder some of us look to storytelling for a semblance of order and structure; some solace, too. I write this in America's hollowed-out, small-town heartland in January 2019 just seven days after hearing voices raised outdoors and looking out my study window to see a 17-year-old boy get shot three times: *pom-pom-pom*. Like I said, chaotic, random, cheap.

Reading plays is seldom a pleasure, because that's not what they're made for. But what can I do but offer up mine in paper and ink?

S.K.M.

AND OTHER PLAYS AND ADAPTATIONS –

AND OTHER PLAYS AND ADAPTATIONS –

A Journal of the Plague Year

Adapted from Daniel Defoe's Book

For Kevin John Bueche
(1957-1993)

A Journal of the Plague Year

(See Introduction for sources.)

CAST OF CHARACTERS

Doubling scheme / Order of appearance

    I. FIDDLER
    E. MARTINDALE
    A. HARRY FOE
    D. TYDINGS
    G. MRS. ASH
    F. JUDITH
    C. JOHN SELKIRK
    H. ASH DAUGHTER
    B. HEATH
    E. WILLIAM FOE
    D. SOLOMON EAGLE
    C. VICTIM
    H. MRS. TYDINGS
    E. GOOD TYDINGS
    F. MOTHER SELKIRK
    G. ESTHER SELKIRK
    E. DICK SELKIRK
    F. QUACK

AND OTHER PLAYS AND ADAPTATIONS –

C. CHARMSELLER
E. COSTERMONGER
C. SIR JOHN LAWRENCE
D. EXAMINER
F. ASH WATCHMAN
C. ASH
C. MARTINDALE WATCHMAN
H. MRS. MARTINDALE
G. NURSE
B. BUCKINGHAM
H. SHOPPER
F. ABRAHAM'S WIDOW
E. THOMAS MOLINS
G. BURIER
F. SEXTON
D. CAPTAIN DAVIS
E. LIMPING MAN
D. PICK
E. ROBERT
G. RACHEL

SCENE AND TIME

A marketplace in London's Whitechapel, May to December of 1665. FOE's house and saddlery (with standing-desk) to one side, TYDINGS' elevated garret to other. ASH and MARTINDALE houses, center.

AT RISE, FIDDLER—improvising on 17th-century dance rhythms throughout—accompanies JUDITH, MRS. ASH and ASH DAUGHTER dancing with silks. FOE, polishing a saddle, converses with TYDINGS.
   Enter MARTINDALE.

MARTINDALE
Mr. Foe? They've disturbed my wife, and she's with child.

FOE [waving FIDDLER to silence]
Sorry, Mr. Martindale.

TYDINGS
How many does this one make, Mr. Martindale?

MARTINDALE
Ten, Mr. Tydings— Ten, indeed, unless—

[Counts on fingers.]

Eleven? I'll ask my wife.

[Exits.]

TYDINGS
Better if his wife did more dancing and less—

[Gestures lewdly. To FIDDLER's mocking *Ring*

> *Around A-Rosy,* MRS. ASH, ASH DAUGHTER and JUDITH dance around TYDINGS.]

Ring Around A-Rosy when the plague is coming?

[Music stops. To FOE:]

Back to business. Selkirk's ship can carry your horse tack out and sugar back for me. The rate for us together will be cheap.

MRS. ASH
Sorry, Mr. Foe, but this woman's goods put us in a mind to dance.

FOE
What kind of goods?

JUDITH
Silks for your wife, sir.

TYDINGS
His *what?*

MRS. ASH
She'll not catch that old bachelor.

FOE
I am a single man, madam.

JUDITH
Your mistress, then. Smooth Levantine silks. Don't tell me your mistress doesn't want a yard? Every woman likes a yard or two.

TYDINGS
Will she take a saddle in exchange?

MRS. ASH
He'll get the softer mount.

JUDITH
I have some — very choice, very rare — that I can show in privacy. Feel this one —

[Enshrouds FOE in silk. HE sneezes. COMPANY flinches.]

But you have work to do. Mistress Ash, you liked the green?

MRS. ASH
Indeed, madam, if you'll come across.

TYDINGS
As I was saying: Selkirk can ship —

FOE
You expect no stop to business?

[Enter JOHN SELKIRK, waving bill.]

TYDINGS
Expecting the worst brings on the worst, that is my experience. Speak of the devil.

FOE
Selkirk, you have it? Well?

JOHN SELKIRK
The bill for this week:

[Reads:]

Deaths, three hundred and forty-two, whereof the plague: seventy-one!

TYDINGS
How many parishes infected?

JOHN SELKIRK
Twelve: Clerkenwell —

JUDITH
Twelve!

JOHN SELKIRK
— Shoreditch, Bishopsgate —

MRS. ASH
Shoreditch? Draws this way from Drury Lane, then.

FOE
Man, what of St. Giles Cripplegate?

JOHN SELKIRK
St. Giles: Deaths, eighteen, whereof the plague: *one*.

FOE
One in our parish!

MRS. ASH
One of our neighbors!

— A JOURNAL OF THE PLAGUE YEAR,

TYDINGS
One only. Still mostly in the west. We're safe here.

JOHN SELKIRK
Though I'll have nothing to do with Shoreditch.

TYDINGS
Or go up Drury Lane — unless upon business.

FOE
I don't know what to do.

TYDINGS
I've no time to anticipate. Selkirk, about that ship —

JOHN SELKIRK
Yes, Tydings — later.

[Exit apart.]

JUDITH [pointing]
Ohh! I see it plain! Ohh!

MRS. ASH
What is it?

FOE
What do you see?

JUDITH
An angel in the sky, clothed in white, a sword of fire in his hand.

MRS. ASH
I see him! He brandishes it over our heads.

ASH DAUGHTER
The sword's plain as can be.

JUDITH
What a glorious face he has!

MRS. ASH
A beautiful face!

FOE
Where? Where do you see him?

JUDITH
Right above. Can you not see?

FOE
No.

ASH DAUGHTER [to MRS. ASH]
What does it mean, Mother?

JUDITH
The meaning of it is, there shall be such a plague in London, the living will not be able to bury the dead! He signs now to the houses. To that house!

[Points at FOE's house.]

The sign of death has been placed on that house.

[HEATH enters, carrying bill.]

Now to the ground.

ASH DAUGHTER
What does that mean, Mother?

JUDITH
That hundreds — thousands — will be buried in that churchyard.

MRS. ASH
I see coffins waiting to be buried! Heaps of dead bodies!

ASH DAUGHTER
Heaps!

JUDITH
Dead! All dead!

[JUDITH, MRS. ASH and ASH DAUGHTER exit.]

FOE
I see — a cloud, bright on one side by the shining of the sun.

HEATH [startling FOE]
So hypochondriac fancies represent
   Ships, armies, battles in the firmament,
Till steady eyes the exhalations solve,
   And all to its first matter — cloud — resolve.

FOE
Heath!

HEATH
Have you seen the bill?

FOE
Neighbor Selkirk brought it.

> HEATH

It has reached the parish. Time you went to the country.

> WILLIAM FOE [entering, waving bill]

Harry, my brother, I've got to talk to you —

> FOE

William! Come in with Doctor Heath.

> SOLOMON EAGLE [off]

Great, most dreadful God!

> [Almost naked spotted VICTIM runs on screaming, dies grotesquely. SOLOMON EAGLE — a plant sprouting from HIS head — follows, circles body.]

> FOE

Is it — ?

> HEATH

Yes. Stay off him.

> FOE

But Christian mercy —

> HEATH

Nothing can be done.

> WILLIAM FOE

Stay off, Harry!

FOE
How do you know it's —?

HEATH
By the mad plunge to outrun the agony.

SOLOMON EAGLE
Oh, the great and the dreadful God! Repent your sins! Repent!

FOE
Stay off me, you crazy Quaker!

SOLOMON EAGLE
Dreadful God!

[Toes VICTIM, at a loss exits.]

WILLIAM FOE
Your first, Harry?

FOE
Yes.

WILLIAM FOE
I saw them in the East — too many of them.

FOE
Did you see the way he kicked?

WILLIAM FOE
Tomorrow I leave for Lincolnshire.

HEATH
Good.

WILLIAM FOE
Brother, come with me. Do not await it here.

FOE
Did you hear the way he screamed?

WILLIAM FOE [producing pamphlet]
Have you looked into *Gadbury's Astrological Predictions*?

HEATH
How can the alignment of planets cause disease?

WILLIAM FOE [producing pamphlet]
Have you read *Come Out of Her, My People, Lest You Partake of Her Plagues*?

HEATH
Did you see that man die? Saddlers are not wanted here.

WILLIAM FOE
Though physicians are.

FOE
All my property in the world is embarked in my business.

HEATH
What is that to saving your life?

FOE
Does not fear make what's coming worse?

WILLIAM FOE
With London ripe for destruction? The king's restored, the city's rich, luxurious and gay. Harry, the one sure preparation is to run away.

HEATH

Foe: The sole antidote is compounded of three adverbs: *Cito, Longe, Tarde* — Fly quickly, go far, return slowly.

WILLIAM FOE

You are with me?

HEATH

Completely.

FOE

But if I flee the Lord's presence —

HEATH

Not His presence: His plague.

FOE

I should trust in God with my health.

WILLIAM FOE

Come with me, Harry.

FOE

I have no horse, and 'tis too late to get one.

WILLIAM FOE

I have a horse. I have a cart.

FOE

I did direct my servant to prepare my journey and he — left me.

HEATH

An intimation from heaven!

FOE
Then I arranged with a woman in my trade to take over my affairs and—

WILLIAM FOE
And?

FOE
She fell ill.

HEATH
Providence!

FOE
I should take my lot where God has placed me.

WILLIAM FOE
In the East I saw the Turks presume upon your notion that every man's end is beforehand decreed. Saw them stay in infected places, converse with infected persons—

FOE
Did you?

WILLIAM FOE
—and die by the heaps. Whereas I, who kept retired and reserved, escaped.

FOE
He can preserve me in the midst of danger.

HEATH
When contagion spreads from the sick to the well?

FOE
No, no, 'tis a stroke from heaven.

HEATH
Not a stroke without the agency of means.

FOE
Heath, you talk like an atheist.

HEATH
Even if the plague be the will of God, 'tis under the conduct of human causes, human effects, and has its specific agent. Everybody receives the infection through secret conveyance after intercourses with the infected. Nor can caution prevent it spreading: Impossible to tell infected people from sound, or that the infected can themselves know, for no symptoms appear until a fit time of maturity.

FOE
"Specific agent"?

HEATH
Steams or fumes we call effluvia. They penetrate the blood, mingling with it and raising the tokens.

FOE
"Tokens"?

HEATH
Spots like flea bites, or larger ones that cover the body, or — the buboes.

FOE
"Buboes"?

WILLIAM FOE
Ghastly, Harry. Ghastly.

HEATH
Swellings in the neck and secret places of armpit and groin. Knobs that cause such pain men leap roaring out of windows.

WILLIAM FOE
I still hear them, Harry — screams and ravings.

FOE
And the course of the disease?

HEATH
It begins with cold shivering like an ague,

[FOE shivers]

then shuddering like burning fever.

[FOE shudders.]

Sweat breaks out as if the body would dissolve. It makes feeble like the palsy, causes madness like the frenzy, and death like a flash of lightning.

WILLIAM FOE
Brother, are you all right?

FOE
But you can treat it?

HEATH
If there are tokens, we cut them, lance them, burn them with caustics —

FOE
A cure?

HEATH
If they can be brought to a head, the patient may recover. But many more poor creatures we torture to death.

WILLIAM FOE
Well, Harry?

FOE
They say it seizes men with the urge to infect others.

HEATH
When men are unconcerned for their own safety, they are careless of others. But purposely communicate the venom? I do not grant the fact.

FOE
William, give me till tomorrow to consider?

WILLIAM FOE
You will resolve?

FOE
I will resolve.

[WILLIAM FOE exits.]

Heath, do you go to the country?

HEATH
No, no, I stay in the city. But you should go.

[Exits.]

FOE

I know not what to do. Lord, you direct me!

> [Kneels, pages through Bible, at random reads Psalm 91:]

"He shall deliver thee from the snare of the fowler and from the noisome pestilence. He shall cover thee with His feathers and under His wings shalt thou trust. Ten thousand shall fall at thy side, but because thou hast made the Lord thy habitation, no plague shall come nigh thy dwelling."

> [Closes Bible.]

You are my refuge, Lord: I shall stay where I dwell.

> [Rises, at desk writes rapidly.]

"It was about the beginning of September 1664 that I, among the rest of my neighbors, heard that the plague was returned again in Holland. Some said it was brought from Africa, others from the Levant among Turkish goods. It seems the Government knew of it, but kept all private and hushed. Hence this rumor died off and people forgot it, as a thing we were little concerned in—" No—

> [scratches paper, writes]

"—as a thing that concerned us not—" No—

> [scratches, writes:]

"—as a thing we hoped was not true"—*yes*—"till two men died in Drury Lane. The Lord Mayor ordered physicians to make inspection. Finding tokens upon the bodies, they gave their opinion that they died of the plague. Whereupon it was printed in the next weekly bill of mortality: Plague, two. Parishes infected, one."

[Continues writing.
TYDINGS enters where sit MRS. TYDINGS and GOOD TYDINGS.]

MRS. TYDINGS
Come, Good, another dainty?

TYDINGS [waving bill]
Mrs. Tydings, our foreign guest has arrived in the parish. We must prepare.

MRS. TYDINGS
We were just talking of it.

GOOD TYDINGS
Yes, sir, they say —

TYDINGS
I have considered whether to stay or go or what. When the bills overtop one thousand a week dead of it —

GOOD TYDINGS
One thousand a week!

MRS. TYDINGS
'Tisn't possible!

TYDINGS
— we will shut ourselves up with all we need for a year.

GOOD TYDINGS
A year!

MRS. TYDINGS
Cannot we go to the country?

GOOD TYDINGS
Let's go to the country, Father.

TYDINGS [preparing quill at table]
To meet the plague there? As to my preparations: silence. If our neighbors Foe or Martindale or Ash learn I am hoarding, then when they starve of their own improvidence— I am writing as for my trade, to have supplies taken roundabout into my warehouse before bringing them privately here.

MRS. TYDINGS
What supplies?

TYDINGS [writing]
I will buy a thousandweight of sea-biscuit bread, put up in hogsheads as for a long voyage.

MRS. TYDINGS
Sea-biscuit bread?

TYDINGS
And what is wrong with sea-biscuit bread?

GOOD TYDINGS
So coarse and uneatable.

TYDINGS

Nonetheless you will eat it: It keeps. However — in addition, I shall get ten barrels of fine flour, packed up as though for Jamaica.

MRS. TYDINGS

Fine flour. Good, I shall bake cakes —

TYDINGS

We cannot live on cakes.

[Writes:]

A fat bullock's flesh pickled. Two barrels thus of pork. Three hundred pound-weight of cheeses: Wiltshire, Gloucestershire, and old Cheshire. Twelve firkins of salt butter. Salt, pickles, neats' tongues, hams, ten stone bottles of oil. Coals, gunpowder, eighty dozen pounds of candles. And medicines: mithridate, Venice treacle, diachylin, *et cetera*.

MRS. TYDINGS

Medicines?

TYDINGS

I'll dig a well in the yard, that we can daily wash every room in the house, and I'll poison the rats and mice and kill our cats and dogs.

[MRS. TYDINGS cries out.]

With due preparations we shall survive — if I am in time to avoid scarcities. I think I am.

MRS. TYDINGS

Do not forget our other needs, husband.

TYDINGS

Other needs?

[Snaps fingers.]

Beer! Say eighteen barrels, well hopped. Not for mirth, son.

GOOD TYDINGS

Oh no, sir, but the physicians order us not to let our spirits sink.

TYDINGS [writing]

Well, and two casks of malmsey, a barrel of malaga sack, two runlets of brandy, and one of this new cordial they call plague water. A most sufficient magazine. I shall bolt and bind and lock us up—even close the chimneys but this one.

[Climbs to garret, calling:]

And install a pulley to let down victuals to the porter he can trust to eat, and his wages, and he shall tell us how it goes with the city.

MRS. TYDINGS [calling]

But always to stay inside?

GOOD TYDINGS [calling]

Nothing to do but watch outdoors?

TYDINGS

Watch outdoors? I will nail our casements shut, except this one, which I will cover with tin that nothing infectious can stick. And this one I shall open only after causing a flash of gunpowder to purify the air coming in. And once we are in, if you offer to stir but a foot outside the door, you shall not come in again. For we shall survive!

                GOOD TYDINGS

I have never before seen my father show fear.

                MRS. TYDINGS

He is not afraid, Good! Don't say such a thing!

            [Calling:]

Mr. Tydings? Let us not neglect our souls. Let us place our trust in the Lord.

            [Screams as TYDINGS sets off
            FLASH of gunpowder, opens
            window amidst smoke.]

                TYDINGS

An excellent idea, Mrs. Tydings!

            [Closes window.
                JOHN SELKIRK, holding
            bill, paces while MOTHER
            SELKIRK and ESTHER
            SELKIRK read missals, DICK
            SELKIRK looks on.]

                JOHN SELKIRK

We must bethink ourselves of what 'tis prudent to do while we have time.

MOTHER SELKIRK

John Selkirk, time has value only so as we prepare for the soul's eternal welfare. That time, once slipped away, is lost forever.

ESTHER SELKIRK

Forever.

MOTHER SELKIRK

Son, you cannot remember the old plagues: In 1635 there died ten thousand, in 1624 above fifty thousand.

DICK SELKIRK

Dreadful, those old times.

MOTHER SELKIRK

Dreadful for those whose eternal state was not secured.

ESTHER SELKIRK

If we fall on our knees together like the people of Ninevah, surely God will repent Him of His anger!

MOTHER SELKIRK

I do not expect it. Things were never worse than now, such debauchery loose among us. "'Shall I not visit for these things?' saith the Lord."

ESTHER SELKIRK

Jeremiah, chapter nine, verse nine.

DICK SELKIRK

The world was as wicked since I remember it.

ESTHER SELKIRK
Your "words seemed to them as idle tales." Luke twenty-four, verse eleven.

JOHN SELKIRK
You make your company melancholy, madam, always harping on this subject.

MOTHER SELKIRK
In 1624 I was full of mirth as you are now, when on a sudden it broke out and turned our smiles to—

JOHN SELKIRK
It came without warning?

MOTHER SELKIRK
Oh no, we had warning, but we were young and when people spoke of repenting, we thought them melancholy.

DICK SELKIRK
Might do some good in London. Thin the rabble.

JOHN SELKIRK [putting bill away]
I suppose 'tis always in one part or another of the city. Besides, everybody is willing to hope they will escape.

MOTHER SELKIRK
Every soldier hopes not to be hit, but puts on his helmet that he may fare the better if he is. Take my word, when it comes you'll say 'tis a time to tremble at, a time to be prepared *for*, not a time to prepare *in*.

JOHN SELKIRK
One only dead in St. Giles, and that doubtful.

MOTHER SELKIRK
When the bill sets down one for plague, eight or ten are dead of it, for people conceal it. 'Tis of utmost consequence not to be known to be infected, for they would not be shunned or have their shops shunned.

JOHN SELKIRK
What, madam, would you have us do?

MOTHER SELKIRK
We must prepare for a dreadful visitation. We must prepare for death.

JOHN SELKIRK
I might send you and Esther to the country. And Dick.

ESTHER SELKIRK
I will prepare for death as if I was actually infected.

DICK SELKIRK [pointing]
Nay, sister, you have it already! I see the tokens upon you!

[ESTHER SELKIRK cries out.]

JOHN SELKIRK
Oh for God's sake—

MOTHER SELKIRK
How can you be so cruel?

DICK SELKIRK
She said she was not frighted at the plague, but only at not being prepared.

ESTHER SELKIRK
Because I am not prepared, I was surprised. But from this hour I look upon myself as infected.

MOTHER SELKIRK
So must we all! Oh, that it frighted the whole nation into the same resolution!

JOHN SELKIRK
This is enough to scare us all to death.

        [Exits.
        FOE writes. Enter JUDITH.]

JUDITH
Silks for your wife, sir?

FOE
I am a single man, madam.

JUDITH
Your mistress, then? Every woman likes a yard or two.

FOE
I have no mistress, madam.

JUDITH
No?

FOE
Another time.

JUDITH
Why not this time?

FOE
I don't know.

JUDITH
I'm sound. Try your luck. I'll try mine.

FOE
I could lose.

JUDITH
Or you could win — me.

FOE
Only to lose you, perhaps.

JUDITH
Another time you might lose me. Why not win me this time?

FOE
Because inside of me is a place black with a kind of plague —

[JUDITH backs away.]

I don't mean that, I'm sound. Only, my heart is discouraged and alone and in the dark —

JUDITH [advancing]
Mine too.

[Pause.]

FOE
I have work to do, madam.

[Exit JUDITH. FOE writes.]

"Like a storm cloud, it now moved eastward towards where I lived. People picked up what they could and fled, the more hastily for the rumor that the government was placing barriers on the roads. Terrors led people running also to fortune-tellers and quacking philosophers who sold ridiculous, useless stuff, their infallible preventive pills—"

          QUACK
Infallible preventive pills against the plague! The universal remedy for the universal plague, too late for some—but not too late for you.

> [MRS. ASH and ASH DAUGHTER listen to QUACK as FOE and HEATH enter, joined by CHARMSELLER, COSTERMONGER and TYDINGS.]

          HEATH [holding bill]
Foe, this week's bill must persuade you to go while still you may.

          FOE
'Tis my duty to stay where I dwell.

          HEATH
Madness! And you, Tydings?

> [Hands bill to TYDINGS, who reads it, puts in pocket.]

          TYDINGS
Perhaps I shall, business drags so. People would rather crowd into church than eat, though a sneeze or bad smell—the

smallest fart—spreads such panic as instantly to clear St. Paul's.

> [CHARMSELLER farts.
> COMPANY scatters, glaring at
> TYDINGS.]

How much do you suppose this charlatan gets?

> QUACK

Mine's true plague water, the royal antidote against infection. My black art cured multitudes last year in Amsterdam—

> HEATH

How will you eat?

> FOE

The God who gave me brains will give me food.

> HEATH

Man, at the least lay in provisions: Bake your own bread, brew your own beer—and keep within doors.

> FOE

That will keep me safe?

> HEATH [handing herbs]

'Tis the utmost you can do. If you must come out, keep garlic or licorice in your mouth.

> QUACK

Incomparable drink against the plague, never found out before—

FOE
Stay in? Not see how the city's faring?

TYDINGS [to QUACK]
Tell me what will become of me?

COSTERMONGER
Will my master keep me? Or leave me to starve?

CHARMSELLER [accosting HEATH]
These cheats spread fear. The authorities should ban them.

HEATH
Perhaps. But it despises medicine. We physicians go about prescribing till we drop down dead.

QUACK
My tinctures will keep you safe! They contain copper, silver and Benzoar stone of the East!

CHARMSELLER
Strange that she omits gold, but that I believe she reserves for her own pockets.

QUACK
I help the poor gratis. That's right, gratis for the poor. Line up there.

[Points to FOE:]

You, sir, right this way.

TYDINGS
I came up first!

QUACK

Wait your turn.

[To FOE:]

This way, sir.

MRS. ASH

You say you help the poor for nothing?

QUACK

My advice I give for nothing—but not my medicine.

TYDINGS

You lay a snare then, advising the poor gratis to buy your physick.

CHARMSELLER

So does every shopkeeper.

QUACK [to FOE]

Sir, you may come up.

[TYDINGS gives coin, takes bottle, exits.]

MRS. ASH

Here now, he's got his, I want mine.

CHARMSELLER [to FOE and HEATH]

You don't want that quack, sirs—petty unperforming thief, bad as the men.

FOE
A disgrace.

CHARMSELLER
At a time when any of us might be tossed into the common grave, what we want is the true antidote.

FOE
You mean place our faith in Him —

CHARMSELLER [producing charm]
That's it: A proven amulet, a charm to keep it off. See the holy *Abracadabra*, the letters forming a pyramid up even to the "A"?

FOE
You should think of your grave, not your purse!

CHARMSELLER
Same to you!

[HEATH laughs.
CHARMSELLER searches
SELF.]

MRS. ASH
What do you laugh at?

FOE
Nothing. We didn't laugh.

ASH DAUGHTER
I saw you laugh, scoffers.

FOE
No, we did not.

ASH DAUGHTER

Profane fellows!

[Enter SOLOMON EAGLE.]

MRS. ASH

If you're infected, buy your own physick! I won't share mine.

[To SOLOMON EAGLE:]

Stay off them!

ASH DAUGHTER

They have it!

SOLOMON EAGLE

They have it! 'Tis a judgment! Great and dreadful God!

FOE

We do not have it — We're sound as you are!

[HEATH hustles FOE across.]

CHARMSELLER [accosting THEM]

If you're papist, this Jesuit cross —

FOE

To hell with your trumpery!

HEATH [grabbing CHARMSELLER's sleeve]

The tokens! Surely to yourself you admit your lies?

[CHARMSELLER runs off.]

People! Don't throw money away on whimsies, but go home, avoid adventurous conduct—

                FOE

Come, Heath.

              MRS. ASH

Whimsies, he calls them!

            COSTERMONGER

You're their rival, ain't you, Doctor Heath?

               HEATH

Don't take poison for physick, death instead of life!

            COSTERMONGER

You're sick and would infect us!

            [COMPANY pelts HEATH and
            FOE with vegetables.]

              MRS. ASH

Unbeliever! *You're* the quack!

            COSTERMONGER

You don't know! Who will keep us alive?

            ASH DAUGHTER

Atheist! Blasphemer!

            SOLOMON EAGLE

Great and dreadful God! God, God, God!

            [Bell tolls. Enter SIR JOHN
            LAWRENCE.]

FOE
As well talk to an east wind, Heath.

SIR JOHN LAWRENCE
Whereas King James gave authority to his Lord Mayor to appoint officers for prevention of infection and relief of those infected, I now order: That examiners be appointed to inquire what persons be sick, and to shut up their houses. That the master of every house, as soon as any one complaineth of blotch or swelling, shall notify the examiner within two hours. That every infected house be shut up for twenty-eight days and marked with a red cross, and each to have a watchman, and that examiners pass the streets holding a red wand three foot in length, evident to be seen. And if any appointed examiner refuse to serve, he shall be committed to prison. That all dogs and cats be killed

[outcry]

and that causes of assembly as rope-dances, bear-baitings and plays be prohibited. May God be with us.

COMPANY
May God be with us.

> [Exit SIR JOHN LAWRENCE, HEATH, SOLOMON EAGLE and QUACK.
> FOE goes to desk as MRS. ASH and ASH DAUGHTER clean up stage.]

ASH DAUGHTER
The town was that quiet when the Lord Mayor spoke, Mother, it had the face of a Sabbath day.

MRS. ASH
A Sabbath better observed than it used to be. What is it, child?

ASH DAUGHTER
A pimple, Mother. I have a pimple on my breast.

MRS. ASH
Sir John's measures will suffice if the poor do not rise up. Still, I am glad of this tonic.

[ASH DAUGHTER vomits.]

Child! What ails you?

ASH DAUGHTER
Oh, my head! My head suddenly aches! Is it—?

MRS. ASH
Don't be silly. Come in.

[Stealthily takes ASH DAUGHTER into ASH house. Screams and cries ensue.]

No! No! Dear God, save us! Husband!

[ASH WATCHMAN and EXAMINER enter, EXAMINER briefly going into ASH house.]

EXAMINER
Shut them up, watchman. Twenty-eight days. Unfortunate people, I found evidence of the plague.

ASH WATCHMAN
Yes, sir!

[EXAMINER exits as ASH WATCHMAN nails cross to door.]

MRS. ASH [at door]
Watchman, 'tis only a child who's ill, and her you may take to the pest house.

ASH WATCHMAN
You know I may not. The examiner has shut up this house.

MRS. ASH
But shut us up and she'll infect us all!

ASH WATCHMAN
I have my instructions.

[FOE notices altercation. Enter MRS. TYDINGS.]

ASH
We are sound people here, yet he shuts us up!

MRS. TYDINGS
What! Watchman, let them out!

COSTERMONGER
Why do you imprison sound people?

MRS. TYDINGS
At this rate we may all be shut away.

COSTERMONGER
Open the house!

ASH WATCHMAN
Nay, I have my instructions.

ASH
Good people, help us. Good neighbor Foe, bring us an axe! Mrs. Tydings, help us.

MRS. ASH
Ten shillings for an axe!

ASH
A pound for two minutes' use of an axe!

COSTERMONGER
An axe! An axe!

ASH WATCHMAN
Get back! This house harbors the plague!

[COSTERMONGER and MRS. TYDINGS exit. FOE returns to desk.]

MRS. ASH
But my children! My children are in here!

ASH
You don't care! Leave us here to die? You'll die too! Every one of you! 'Tis the end to London!

MRS. ASH
The devil's taken London! God save us.

[HEATH and EXAMINER emerge from MARTINDALE house.]

HEATH
I tell you, this distemper is something else. You have no right to shut up this house.

EXAMINER
Not alone the right, but the sworn duty. Watchman, shut it up.

MARTINDALE WATCHMAN
Yes, sir!

[Nails cross to door.]

HEATH
The only one not well in the Martindale house was the prentice, and he only had fever, and now he is well again.

EXAMINER
I hope we are in time to staunch the infection from spreading.

HEATH
There can be no spreading, because there is no infection!

MARTINDALE [at door]
Doctor Heath, what is your judgment?

HEATH
Sir, the threat is less to your health than to your patience. This officious gentleman insists upon shutting you up—

EXAMINER
My clear duty — I do not say a happy one —

HEATH
You see how it lies.

EXAMINER
Duty done satisfies everyone.

[Exits.]

MRS. MARTINDALE
For how long?

HEATH
Twenty-eight days, Mrs. Martindale.

MARTINDALE
Well, we have food. Might be safer, shut away.

MRS. MARTINDALE
We will make shift.

[HEATH exits.
TYDINGS opens window
with FLASH of gunpowder.]

TYDINGS [calling]
Abraham. Abraham! I am shutting up now. Stay at my door and I shall let down your food every day and wages on Saturday.

[Closes window, carries bill downstairs.]

Madam, this week's bill: Burials last week—

                MRS. TYDINGS

I heard it was going off.

                TYDINGS

In Aldgate, Stepney, Whitechapel—

                GOOD TYDINGS

Please, Father.

                TYDINGS

This fourteenth of July the bill amounts to one thousand, seven hundred and sixty-two—

                GOOD TYDINGS

Whereof—?

                TYDINGS

Better ask, whereof *not*? Fifteen hundred dead of plague! Doubled in one week!

                MRS. TYDINGS

The authorities have the situation in hand, Mr. Tydings, shutting up houses and—

                TYDINGS

Mistress Tydings, the—plague—is—begun!

                MRS. TYDINGS

Yes, Mr. Tydings, but let me go out, there is one thing I must do.

                TYDINGS [going upstairs]

By all means, but who goes out now may not return.

GOOD TYDINGS
Mother, he cannot treat us thus.

MRS. TYDINGS
He thinks it best, Good.

GOOD TYDINGS
Have you tasted sea-biscuit bread?

MRS. TYDINGS
Sailors eat it.

GOOD TYDINGS
We are not sailors, nor are we infected: We are shut up causelessly.

TYDINGS [calling]
I will take no chances. None. If I have anything to do with it, we shall survive.

[Opens window with FLASH of gunpowder, MRS. TYDINGS screaming. Peers out, closes window.]

ASH
Watchman. Watchman!

ASH WATCHMAN
Yo.

ASH
Fetch a nurse! Quick, man!

ASH WATCHMAN
Are you sick?

ASH
'Tis my daughter, she's worse.

ASH WATCHMAN
Well? What can I do about it?

ASH
Fetch a nurse! By law you must do our necessary errands, and fetching a keeper is a Christian necessary!

ASH WATCHMAN
Oh, all right, all right.

[Exits.]

MRS. ASH
Now hurry!

[ASH flinging down cross, he and MRS. ASH run off.
ASH WATCHMAN enters with NURSE.]

ASH WATCHMAN
What the—! Zounds!

NURSE
Have your birds flown?

ASH WATCHMAN [to FOE at desk]
Sir, did you see this?

[Coughing, FOE turns away.
ASH WATCHMAN and
NURSE enter ASH house.]

BUCKINGHAM [off]

Bring out your dead!

[Pushes dead-cart on.]

Bring out your dead!

NURSE

Dead here!

[BUCKINGHAM halts. ASH
WATCHMAN and NURSE
place ASH DAUGHTER's
body in dead-cart, NURSE
taking ring.]

BUCKINGHAM

'Ere, give that ring to me.

NURSE

I saw it first.

ASH WATCHMAN

Half the value's mine.

NURSE

Mine. You never saw it.

BUCKINGHAM

Give it over.

NURSE [indicating body]
No, you don't, that's your prize.

[Exits bickering with ASH
WATCHMAN.]

BUCKINGHAM
No wonder they call nurses keepers: Whatever they gets, they keeps. Ah, you're a pretty wench.

[Fondling body, pushes dead-
cart off.]

Bring out your dead!

[FOE writes. JUDITH enters.]

FOE
Silk seller! How d'you fare? Come closer —

JUDITH
I go this way.

FOE
Come closer. Perhaps I wish to cheapen your silks.

JUDITH
Then you are out of luck, for of silks I have none, not since they stopped the shipping.

FOE
How do you live?

JUDITH
What's it to you?

FOE
I don't mean—

JUDITH
I know what you mean, what men always mean.

FOE [approaching]
No.

JUDITH [backing away]
Stay off me. Go back to your writing. Why do you write? Does writing stop it? No. Ease anyone's suffering? No. Save your friends? No!

FOE
My friends are where, if not here? If I can tell our story in accents that alarm the soul, I shall rejoice that I see these things and remember them.

JUDITH
I don't want to remember. I want to forget!

[Exits.]

FOE
Damn!

[Resumes writing.
FLASH as TYDINGS opens window.]

TYDINGS
Abraham! Abraham! Abraham!

ABRAHAM'S WIDOW [entering]

Abraham is dead, sir.

TYDINGS

Who are you?

ABRAHAM'S WIDOW

His widow, sir.

TYDINGS

His—?

ABRAHAM'S WIDOW

I woke up this morning and found his jaw was fallen and his eyes were open. He was almost cold, sir.

TYDINGS

Why did you come out?

ABRAHAM'S WIDOW

I knew you would want him.

TYDINGS

But if he is dead, I must want him. You cannot help me, nor I you.

ABRAHAM'S WIDOW [holding out arms]

Oh sir, I am provided for—marked with the tokens. I shall not be long after my Abraham. In his place I have brought you an honest man.

[Enter THOMAS MOLINS.]

TYDINGS
How do I know he's not infected?

ABRAHAM'S WIDOW
He is one of the safe men, sir. He had it and recovered, so he cannot get it again.

TYDINGS [tossing coin]
Take this.

ABRAHAM'S WIDOW
Thank you, sir.

TYDINGS
Tell me, why have the bells stopped? Is it almost finished?

ABRAHAM'S WIDOW
Why, the number that die is so great, they forbid the ringing of bells on anybody.

THOMAS MOLINS
The very bells are hoarse with tolling.

TYDINGS
Well, and what is this cry we hear but cannot make out?

ABRAHAM'S WIDOW
Cry?

TYDINGS
Every night, lately in the day as well. A man passes, bawling.

THOMAS MOLINS
I know, master: *Bring out your dead!*

[TYDINGS closes window
firmly.]

Bring out your dead! Bring out your dead!

[Settles beneath window.
ABRAHAM'S WIDOW exits.
HEATH emerges from
MARTINDALE house.]

MRS. MARTINDALE [at door]
Air is what I need, to walk in the sun.

HEATH
You shall have your freedom, Mrs. Martindale.

[EXAMINER emerges.]

You see there never was plague in this house.

EXAMINER
Last time I was wrong, I admit it, but 'tis a different matter now.

HEATH

What?

EXAMINER
The woman is scorbutic.

HEATH
Lack of air and exercise. Free them.

EXAMINER
Watchman, twenty-eight days more.

                HEATH
No!

        MARTINDALE WATCHMAN
Yes, sir!

        [Nails cross to door.]

                HEATH
Death and damnation!

            MARTINDALE
Doctor Heath?

             EXAMINER
I have my duty. If in four weeks she improves —

         [Staggers.]

              HEATH
How can she improve, when you shut her up?

             EXAMINER
Doctor Heath, attend: What's the matter with me?

        [HEATH peels back
        EXAMINER's shirt.]

              HEATH
You are a dead man. Pray you have not killed this family.

            MARTINDALE
What is it? What's the matter?

         MRS. MARTINDALE
Doctor Heath?

[EXAMINER staggers off.
FOE staggers on.]

FOE

Heath! How d'you fare?

HEATH

Foe? Told you to stay close —

FOE

Behold me a living monument of the Almighty's protection.

HEATH

Go in again.

FOE

I cannot quell my curiosity. I come back frighted, yet I cannot stay home. Indeed, I must see to my brother's hats in Swan Alley, for he left them in my care.

[HEATH exits, shaking head.]

NURSE [off, gaily]

Oh, death! Death! Death!

[Enters with SHOPPER, BOTH wearing multiple hats, carrying more.]

FOE

What business have you with these, mistress?

NURSE

No more than she.

FOE
What were you doing at William Foe's warehouse? Give me those hats!

NURSE
They're not for you!

SHOPPER [hatting FOE]
Oh yes, very becoming indeed. Ain't he pretty?

FOE
I shall lock you in and fetch the constable.

NURSE [revealing bandaged face]
That's right, lock up and come in with me. We'll have a toss.

FOE
Away! Get away from me!

[Slowly collapses. NURSE and SHOPPER exit laughing while BUCKINGHAM pushes on dead-cart, SOLOMON EAGLE, draped in gold, standing triumphant atop it.]

SOLOMON EAGLE
There he is, Buckingham! There's our prey: The untouchable, the safe Harry Foe at last!

BUCKINGHAM
I'd rather find a nice dead wench.

FOE
Me? Me? But I'm clean! I must be!

SOLOMON EAGLE
Clean? You can't know, and I don't believe it!

FOE
Who are you?

SOLOMON EAGLE
I am the plague, come to eat you up! I am famished for men!

[Takes hold of FOE.]

FOE [offering pages]
But my journal.

SOLOMON EAGLE [scattering pages]
A journal-keeper, are we? Let's scatter your dead leaves!

BUCKINGHAM [helping FOE onto cart]
Come with me. 'Tis easy, I do everything. That's it, always room for one more.

[On cart, JUDITH sits up.]

FOE
You!

JUDITH
And you.

FOE
We'll be together.

JUDITH [embracing BUCKINGHAM]
I'm with him now. I offered myself to you, but you —

BUCKINGHAM
Aye, women like a man who knows what he likes.

FOE
Please let's go back. I don't want to die!

BUCKINGHAM
You? You don't want to live — hiding your heart away like a jewel.

SOLOMON EAGLE
'Tis the only part of you not infected, Harry Foe.

BUCKINGHAM
Call that living? Your kind's the bulk of my trade.

FOE
But I have no heart!

JUDITH
He speaks the truth.

SOLOMON EAGLE
Lie down, Harry, and shut up.

FOE
Thank you, I think I prefer to wait.

[Climbs down.]

You don't hinder me?

BUCKINGHAM
How? Life's not my domain.

FOE
Jump out! He can't hinder you!

JUDITH
Let's go on now.

BUCKINGHAM
Patience, my pretty.

SOLOMON EAGLE
What's your hurry? You've all eternity.

BUCKINGHAM [pushing dead-cart off]
Bring out your dead! Bring out your dead!

SOLOMON EAGLE
Back for you later, my dainty morsel! Oh dreadful God! Dreadful!

[FOE picks up pages as HEATH enters. Sounds of digging.]

HEATH
Foe!

FOE [jumping in fright]
I feel very well.

HEATH [hand to FOE's brow]
Come along home. I'll take you home.

FOE
Wait—

— A JOURNAL OF THE PLAGUE YEAR,

[BURIER and SEXTON shovel towards FOE.]

BURIER
You're early, gentlemen. Not open for business yet.

FOE
Oh Heath, what a terrible pit.

HEATH
Foe, let's go home.

BURIER
Help us, sir. Measure us your length. Lie down here, sir, for one moment.

FOE
Full forty foot in length, fifteen or sixteen broad, and — nine foot deep, do you make it?

HEATH
About that.

BURIER
Will be twenty, unless the water prevents us.

SEXTON
The water comes at seventeen or eighteen foot, Mr. Foe, and with the order to leave no bodies within six foot, it's dig, dig, dig.

FOE
Do you mean to bury the parish in this dreadful gulf?

BURIER

This hole? Couple days' worth. When 'tis stuffed full, we extend that way.

SEXTON

No, first over to the porch, then down—

BURIER [pointing at FOE]

Look! Death's in his face!

SEXTON

Keep digging. Dig, dig, dig!

[THEY resume digging.
HEATH escorts FOE
across.]

FOE

Heath, 'tis admirable how the authorities do. God keeps *me*, but their civil measures have sense, keeping the streets clear of dead bodies—

HEATH

Removed like dung, in the night.

FOE

And my Lord Mayor will not quit the city, no, he refuses, and built himself a platform on purpose to hear complaints at a safe distance.

HEATH

My Lord Mayor does much, but the dead-cart does more.

FOE [delirious]
Heath, on the other side of the grave we shall be brethren again: Why cannot we join heart and hand on this side?

HEATH
'Tis to be lamented.

FOE
But my notes?

HEATH
At home.

FOE
First I must go and see whereof to write —

HEATH
This way, Foe.

FOE
Death! I mean Heath! I am a dead man!

HEATH
You are not.

FOE
I'm sick!

HEATH [wiping FOE's face]
Men still fall sick of other things. You have fever. I'll put you to bed and bathe your head with vinegar.

[HEATH settling HIM, FOE recites Psalm 23:]

FOE

Heath, the Lord is my shepherd, I shall not want.
He maketh me to lie down in green pastures:
He leadeth me beside the still waters.
Yea, though I walk through the valley of the shadow of death,
I will fear no evil, for thou art with me,
Thy rod and thy staff—they comfort me.

> [Kneeling, MOTHER SELKIRK
> and ESTHER SELKIRK flank
> DICK SELKIRK, who holds
> open Bible.]

DICK SELKIRK

Time is lapsed, death is at the door, and I have an ocean of sins to launch through.

ESTHER SELKIRK

If deferring repentance to the last gasp renders it suspect, yet it may be sincere.

MOTHER SELKIRK

Many a criminal is forgiven even at the gallows.

JOHN SELKIRK [entering]

I have tomorrow's bill. We must make up our minds. In St. Giles alone—

MOTHER SELKIRK

How do you have tomorrow's bill?

JOHN SELKIRK

'Tis brought to my Lord Mayor beforehand.

DICK SELKIRK
What, that they may alter the numbers?

JOHN SELKIRK
How can you say that?

DICK SELKIRK
I take nothing on faith — save for Jesus Christ my Savior.

JOHN SELKIRK
I was asleep not to lay in provisions.

ESTHER SELKIRK
We are all appointed to die, and after death to judgment.

JOHN SELKIRK
Esther, kindly ring no knells over us before we are dead.

DICK SELKIRK
Nay, sister, tell us, what is our duty?

JOHN SELKIRK
Why, you are as bad as she is.

DICK SELKIRK
Bad? Would I were as good.

ESTHER SELKIRK
We must learn to die at the feet of Christ as penitents.

MOTHER SELKIRK
"For the day of the Lord is great and very terrible."

DICK SELKIRK
The Book of— The Book of—

ESTHER SELKIRK
The Book of Joel, chapter two, verse two.

DICK SELKIRK
Chapter two, verse two.

MOTHER SELKIRK
The words of God Himself.

DICK SELKIRK
'Tis a call to us.

ESTHER SELKIRK
Directed to me.

DICK SELKIRK
To me in particular.

ESTHER SELKIRK
To *me*.

JOHN SELKIRK
The words of Job: "Though He slay me, yet will I trust in Him."

MOTHER SELKIRK, DICK SELKIRK, ESTHER SELKIRK
Hallelujah! Amen!

[Exit John Selkirk.]

DICK SELKIRK
Sister, what means Eight John fifty-one, that the faithful shall not see death?

ESTHER SELKIRK

That means death eternal. Natural death is not death, but only a change.

DICK SELKIRK

Madam, at a time when we see this — *change* — marching towards us, perhaps we ought to listen to my brother?

MOTHER SELKIRK

Now, son, when our graves open their mouths, we may rejoice that we believe.

JOHN SELKIRK [rushing in]

Madam! Esther! Dick! God has accomplished my preparations at last!

MOTHER SELKIRK

Thank you, Lord, for delivering this prodigal.

DICK SELKIRK

He means as to removing ourselves. Quick work, John.

MOTHER SELKIRK

I'll not be moved but to heaven.

ESTHER SELKIRK

Amen!

MOTHER SELKIRK

Come, my sons, let us pray!

DICK SELKIRK

John won't pray.

JOHN SELKIRK [kneeling]

Forgive my brother, Lord, his distrust of Thee and me!

MOTHER SELKIRK, ESTHER SELKIRK

Amen!

JOHN SELKIRK

And we thank Thee, Lord, for giving us in Captain Davis the means of surviving Thy righteous work of sweeping London with vengeance, purifying it for—for—

ESTHER SELKIRK

—for the habitation of Thy faithful.

MOTHER SELKIRK

Who is Captain Davis?

JOHN SELKIRK [calling]

Captain Davis?

[Enter CAPTAIN DAVIS.]

Madam, his coming is our deliverance.

MOTHER SELKIRK

How so?

CAPTAIN DAVIS

Have I not landed a ship? And is she not yours, except the sixteenth mine by your friendship? And has she not provisions aboard for twenty men for five months, but can take in no goods, for nobody can ship off anything?

JOHN SELKIRK

To the ship!

ESTHER SELKIRK
We're not ready!

DICK SELKIRK
I think— I think the Lord will forgive us if—

MOTHER SELKIRK
Let us pray—

JOHN SELKIRK
Tomorrow, madam: Captain Davis has appointed tomorrow a fast day— A week's strict fast begins on board ship *tomorrow.*

MOTHER SELKIRK
Captain Davis, is this so?

JOHN SELKIRK [prompting DAVIS]
A bread and water fast.

CAPTAIN DAVIS
Aye, madam, a bread and water fast.

MOTHER SELKIRK
In that case— In that case, I commit myself unto His hands: "The preparation of the heart is from the Lord."

ESTHER SELKIRK
Proverbs, chapter sixteen, verse one—

[JOHN SELKIRK pulls HER off after MOTHER SELKIRK, CAPTAIN DAVIS and DICK SELKIRK following.

> COMPANY enters between
> ASH and MARTINDALE
> houses.]

> FOE [writing]

"My fever abating, I was left with the need and desire to give thanks — and to look for my friend, the silk seller."

> [Joins COMPANY.]

I therefore crowded with my neighbors into St. Giles Church — joined them in a pious service of prayers, sermons, and eulogies of those who had died.

> [To MARTINDALE
> WATCHMAN:]

Have you seen the silk seller?

> MARTINDALE WATCHMAN

The silk seller?

> FOE

Why did I put her off before?

> MARTINDALE WATCHMAN

I thought you knew, Mr. Foe. The silk seller's — gone.

> BUCKINGHAM

Our town has become Golgotha, the place of the skull! We have placed our faith in the Lord!

> FOE

I heard how many friends I lost that week while exchanging uneasy glances with those pressing about me, some coughing,

— A JOURNAL OF THE PLAGUE YEAR,

others scratching or sneezing, and when it came time to sing the Psalm of thanksgiving, my lips gave their service while my legs carried me out again. My knees were shaking.

[Crosses, meets JUDITH.]

You! I thought — too late!

JUDITH
Who knows? Still sound?

FOE
Who knows? There's a kind of — call it plague — inside me.

JUDITH [fondling FOE]
What kind is that? Oh yes, I know this kind.

[THEY kiss. FOE backs HER onto dead-cart and mounts HER while COMPANY sings Psalm 124:]

COMPANY
If it had not been the Lord who was on our side,
  when men rose up against us:
Then they had swallowed us up quick,
  when their wrath kindled against us:
Then the waters had overwhelmed us,
  the stream had gone over our soul:
Blessed be the Lord, who hath not giv'n us as a prey to their teeth.
Our soul is escaped as a bird out of the snare of the fowlers:
    The snare is broken, and we are escaped.
Our help is in the name of the Lord, who made heaven and hell.

[COMPANY disperses,
JUDITH hurrying off while
FOE comfortably makes HIS
way home.
  FLASH at TYDINGS'
window. Lowers bucket.]

TYDINGS
Porter! Porter! Molins!

MARTINDALE WATCHMAN
The man that stood at your door, sir, is dead of the plague.

TYDINGS
Him I had first is dead, but this is the new man.

MARTINDALE WATCHMAN
Called Thomas Molins, was he not?

TYDINGS
No. . . That's right, Molins.

MARTINDALE WATCHMAN
'Tis him I mean.

TYDINGS
Why, that cannot be. He had it before, he cannot have it again. I merely wish the latest bill, and to know how fares the Court at Oxford.

MARTINDALE WATCHMAN
Some have it three, four times that afterwards die of it. They carried poor Tom Molins to the pit last night. As for the king and his court, it has not so much as touched them — thank God! Here's the latest bill, sir — if you have some silver.

— A JOURNAL OF THE PLAGUE YEAR,

                TYDINGS [tossing coin]
Oh all right. Fire it first.

                MARTINDALE WATCHMAN
That I will.

                [Pours powder into bucket,
                fires it, holds paper in smoke.]

                TYDINGS
Now vinegar.

                MARTINDALE WATCHMAN
Yes, sir.

                [Sprinkles paper with vinegar.
                TYDINGS raises bucket.
                    Enter GOOD TYDINGS.]

                TYDINGS
Half burned. What I can make out: Dead of plague this week, eight thousand, two hundred and fifty-two.

                GOOD TYDINGS
No improvement at all?

                TYDINGS
Improvement? Why, yes: Of cancer, there died but one. Of apoplexy, I make out two only. Of grief—no, not one.

                [GOOD TYDINGS causes
                FLASH.]

Close that window, sir.

GOOD TYDINGS
Not yet, sir, I want to look—

TYDINGS
No, sir. There is nothing to be seen, save that grass grows in the very street.

GOOD TYDINGS
Please, sir.

TYDINGS
Please yourself. I care not.

[Collapses.]

GOOD TYDINGS
Father! Mother!

MRS. TYDINGS [entering]
Husband! Give us more air, Good. Husband, we cannot endure confinement longer: No air, no exercise, no greens, no fruits.

TYDINGS
You would plunge out of doors—and die?

MRS. TYDINGS
To stay in is to die.

TYDINGS
I have read that on long sea voyages the juice of the lime is efficacious. You will find among my stores a barrel of it. We will drink of it daily—

— A JOURNAL OF THE PLAGUE YEAR,

GOOD TYDINGS
Have you tasted lime juice?

TYDINGS
—with sugar.

GOOD TYDINGS
Thank you, Father.

TYDINGS
Do not fret, madam. We are one thousand miles from London.

MRS. TYDINGS
He's out of his head!

GOOD TYDINGS
He has captained us thus far in safety, Mother. I will continue our voyage—for we shall survive.

[Causes FLASH, looks out, closes window. Enter SIR JOHN LAWRENCE. FOE drops to one knee, rebuffs red wand.]

FOE
But Lord Mayor—

SIR JOHN LAWRENCE
Mr. Foe—

FOE
To shut up the well with the ill is a kind of murder. It doesn't answer.

SIR JOHN LAWRENCE
But evidently you do.

FOE
'Tis hard to make me go against my judgment.

SIR JOHN LAWRENCE
I know you will do your duty as examiner.

[FOE accepts wand. Exit SIR JOHN LAWRENCE. LIMPING MAN tipsily accosts FOE.]

LIMPING MAN
Harry Foe, in the city? They told me you got out.

FOE
They say the country's worse than the city. I stay safe here.

LIMPING MAN
I'm a sound man, too, and I will tell you why. Oh — the red stick.

FOE
My Lord Mayor summoned me to the Hall.

LIMPING MAN
Oh — the Hall.

FOE
Summoned me to swear me — to make me condemn to death those who are infected by shutting them up.

LIMPING MAN
Well?

FOE
Shutting up houses does not work. People fall ill at a greater rate than ever.

LIMPING MAN
Well, each must do what he can.

FOE
There's nothing I can do. I know people say God can keep us in the midst of danger —

LIMPING MAN
You say that.

FOE
So said thousands who have gone into the pit. I don't know whether you wish to earn any extra —

LIMPING MAN
In the way I think you mean? Not I, thank you.

[Enter ASH.]

Why, 'tis Mr. Ash. Come in, sir, welcome. We have not seen you this long while. Sit you down. Wife! Refreshment for Mr. Ash and Mr. Foe. And for me.

[Absently rubs leg.]

FOE
Well, sir, and your soundness? What preserves you?

LIMPING MAN
Why, when danger threatens, I unbutton my cordial!

> [Unbuttons leather cordial-
> bottle, takes swig.]

And that is why I am a well man today.

> [Offers to FOE, who refuses,
> and to ASH, who takes swig.]

FOE
But how do you know when danger threatens, when no man can see it?

LIMPING MAN [rubbing leg]
I praise the king.

FOE
We all may praise the king.

LIMPING MAN
Aye, but you did not fall at Naseby fighting for the king's father.

FOE
Well?

LIMPING MAN
Why, when I'm in company with those who are infected, be they sound to all appearance, my old wound smarts.

> [Rubbing leg, rises.]

I then rise up and say: Friends, somebody in this room has the plague! And that breaks up the company, and that prevents infection, and I turn to my cordial and —

[Takes swig, sits down.]

Mr. Ash, you are quiet.

ASH

I am come to take my leave of you.

LIMPING MAN

Where are you going?

ASH

Going? Why, to my long house. I shall die tomorrow night. I have got the plague.

[LIMPING MAN and FOE leap away.]

Are you disturbed at me? Why then, I'll go home and die there.

[Exit ASH.]

LIMPING MAN

Wife! Burn pitch and gunpowder and sulphur! But not together! And scrub down the walls! And wash my clothes! I knew it! I knew it!

[Limps off, scrambling out of clothes. FOE goes to MARTINDALE house.]

MARTINDALE WATCHMAN
Twenty-eight days already, sir?

FOE
How do they?

MARTINDALE WATCHMEN
Don't think on me, I can find another post in a minute.

MARTINDALE [at door]
Mr. Examiner, free us. 'Tis death to shut us in longer!

MRS. MARTINDALE
Death!

FOE
First I must inspect.

[MARTINDALE and MRS. MARTINDALE display THEMSELVES.]

MRS. MARTINDALE
I am well, Mr. Foe.

FOE
Happy to see it, Mrs. Martindale.

MARTINDALE
I am well also, Mr. Foe.

FOE
So you are, Mr. Martindale.

MARTINDALE
But we need sunshine, fresh air.

[Groan within.]

FOE
Man, you have plague in this house! It must be shut up again!

MARTINDALE
No! You kill us!

MRS. MARTINDALE
He's only a servant boy!

FOE
I must! I'm sworn to!

[To MARTINDALE WATCHMAN:]

Twenty-eight days more.

MARTINDALE WATCHMAN
Aye, sir, twenty-eight days it is.

MARTINDALE
You son of a bitch, Foe. Bloody whoreson shitsack!

MRS. MARTINDALE
Dung for the dungheap!

MARTINDALE
I hope it gets you and you die in agony. Agony!

MRS. MARTINDALE
I see plague sores on you! Running with dirty pus! *Pah!*

[Spits.]

MARTINDALE
You're for the worms, Harry Foe! For the worms!

[Crossing, FOE meets PICK.]

PICK
Well, well: the red stick. And how many of you here in St. Giles, Mr. Foe?

FOE
Eighteen examiners in St. Giles alone, Mr. Pick.

PICK
I don't envy you, going into infected places.

FOE
Oh, that is no concern, with the precautions Doctor Heath enjoins upon me, not that I presume to dictate to Him above —

PICK
Amen, amen, His will be done. What precautions?

FOE
Garlic and licorice are sovereign against it.

PICK
Everyone knows that.

FOE
No, 'tis necessary work, Mr. Pick, for our safety depends upon shutting up the sick, but my business needs attention, so I want to find a neighbor to take my place.

PICK
You should shut up all the sick, all who converse promiscuously with the sick, and all who are infected, and be done with it. Do that and no sound person could fall ill.

FOE
But 'tis propagated insensibly, Mr. Pick, by those not visibly infected.

PICK
Self-preservation is the first law, Mr. Foe. They should be shut up, shut up and watched — for they break out, you know.

FOE
I know.

PICK
Well, and does any emolument attach to this office?

FOE
No —

PICK
Oh, well, then.

FOE
— but in gratitude to a man willing to fill my place, I shall reward him ten pounds.

PICK
Ten pounds?

FOE
Ten guineas, Mr. Pick.

PICK
Still I wonder how safe can it be, day in, day out, to go near the sick?

FOE
You might as well ask, is it safe here?

PICK
Oh, we are secure here. I have been cautious since the first rumor. I have not come near anyone sick all this time. Not one.

FOE
Hard to say, when men alive and well one hour are dead the next.

PICK
That is true, but I have not been with any person there has been any danger in. Not one.

FOE
No? Was not you at the Bull Head Tavern with Mr. Heyward night before last?

PICK
Yes, I was, but there was nobody dangerous there. Why, Mr. Heyward is not dead, is he?

[FOE rises.]

Then I am a dead man too.

FOE
I must shut you up, Mr. Pick.

[Leads PICK off.]

— A JOURNAL OF THE PLAGUE YEAR,

              BUCKINGHAM [pushing dead-cart on]

Bring out your dead! Bring out your dead!

              [Weeping NURSE sets down tiny coffin, exits.]

What's this—firewood?

              [Dumps body in cart and breaks coffin, lofts lumber.]

Faggots! Faggots! Five for sixpence, good green faggots!

              MARTINDALE WATCHMAN

Dead here!

              BUCKINGHAM [knocking]

Bring out your dead, bring out your dead!

              [Helps MARTINDALE WATCHMAN load MRS. MARTINDALE's body. MARTINDALE follows.
    Meanwhile, followed by BUCKINGHAM, FOE crosses to where SEXTON and BURIER dig.]

              FOE

Sexton—

              SEXTON

Mr. Foe?

FOE
Admit me, Sexton: I am pressed in my mind to see what might be an instructing sight.

SEXTON
Nay then, name of God, come in. 'Twill be a sermon to you, for 'tis a speaking sight. Burier, you missed a foot.

[MARTINDALE wails.]

BURIER
Made him walk, did you? Refused him the last ride?

BUCKINGHAM
Nay, he is sound, only I have his wife and children.

MARTINDALE [kneeling]
My wife. My children.

SEXTON
Now don't stay here.

BUCKINGHAM
Some girls in here, Sexton, virgin till now, if I don't mistake.

SEXTON
And for eternity, Mr. Buckingham. Into my pit you cannot come.

BUCKINGHAM
Saving them for yourself?

[Pushes dead-cart off.]

MARTINDALE
My wife! My children!

SEXTON
In the pit, are they?

BURIER
Why don't you leap in the pit? Leap on your wife and go to heaven?

FOE
Cannot you see the man's sorrow? Decent men should respect it.

BURIER
You be quiet.

SEXTON
And why are you not at home praying against the dead-cart?

BURIER
Mayhap 'tis too late: He looks peaked and blotchy.

SEXTON
He's for our pit in earnest.

FOE
I am preserved that I might prevent you jeering at a man whom death makes mute and disconsolate.

MARTINDALE
Why, 'tis Mr. Examiner. 'Tis Harry Foe!

FOE
I speak calmly from consciousness of what is due a merciful God—

MARTINDALE
'Tis *you* made my family sick! *You* put my wife and my children into the pit!

BURIER
Preach at *us*, will you!

SEXTON
Marked out special by God?

BURIER
Call upon your God?

[SEXTON and BURIER attack FOE, who flees, pulling MARTINDALE.]

FOE [kneeling]
I mind not your drollery, for I know He will single you out. Though 'tis no certain rule to judge of anyone's eternal state by their dying of plague, I know He will not spare enemies that insult and mock Him, but will tumble them into the muck pit, undermost of all, bruised and pressed with tenscore dead above!

MARTINDALE
No! 'Tis not His judgment on my good wife, my sweet babies! Not so! Not so!

[Pummels unresisting FOE, scatters manuscript, exits.

HEATH enters as FOE
picks up pages, breaks wand
on knee.]

FOE
Ah, Heath, I got your summons. A welcome prospect
company is, too, for around us only death. We draw in death
when we breathe. I need an evening's refuge.

HEATH
There is no refuge from London's hell, unless journal-writing
be prophylactic.

FOE
It takes me away from the horrors I have seen. That is, permits
me to face them, for a time.

HEATH
And you write them down?

FOE
I cannot stop myself. I look and write, look closer and write
more.

HEATH
You have seen what is not good to see, but good to remember.

FOE
Nothing that everyone does not see.

HEATH
You perceive it in its parts and proportions. 'Tis yours to tell
the story of this time that is not to be paralleled in history.

FOE
Write how God betrayed us, and ignored us, played with us, abandoned us?

HEATH
Write it down.

FOE
How some die and others live?

HEATH
Put it down, what it was when it happened.

FOE
'Tis no chronicle of two kings jousting.

HEATH
No, not of two kings.

FOE
Nor of men fighting in battle for their nation.

HEATH
True, no human enemy's engaged.

FOE
Nor is it the story of a man and woman.

HEATH
Nor yet of a man and woman.

FOE
'Tis a story of nothing but fear and sickness and death, of loss without shape, without meaning, without solace, without end.

— A JOURNAL OF THE PLAGUE YEAR,

HEATH

That's it. Let it not be without remembrance, however. Write it down, Foe: A plague's the proper mirror for mankind. I have been more fortunate than you in laying down my responsibility.

FOE

How do you mean?

HEATH

I am within the two hours, I think.

FOE

Did I mistake my time?

HEATH

So soon as the tokens appeared, I sent to you.

FOE

Is it your servant? I will find her space in the pest house, I swear it—

HEATH

'Tis not my servant.

FOE

Not your wife—?

HEATH

Not my wife.

FOE

Thank God. Who then?

HEATH
The young men teach me, Foe. They are strangely borne up against the disease, less troubled themselves than others are troubled for them. This morning I attended a sweet, loving youth. In his sickness he had much quiet upon his spirit. He lay so unconcerned that I marveled, and he went away to his father's house with great peace. I could not blame the mother's grief for the loss of such a son, but to be immoderate was not well. Now 'tis time to dry up tears and lay aside sorrow for those filled with joy in the heavenly mansions.

[Produces walnut.]

And I have this.

FOE
What's that?

HEATH
A walnut filled with quicksilver.

FOE
You called such charms superstition.

HEATH
Against miasmata invisible, effluvia unseen? They must live floating upon the air, in the interstices of the aerial particles, conveyed from one to another as words are conveyed from mouth to ear, by the vibration of the air. I wrote this out for you.

[Holds out receipt.]

I took it just now with great relief.

FOE [reading]
"Take burnt hartshorn half an ounce, the black tops of crabs' claws an ounce and a half" —

HEATH
You may take it with more faith than unicorn's horn, which at five pounds the ounce only the rich may buy — What a sink of filthiness is the body of man. The sink and receptacle of filth. No wonder He has had His fill of us.

FOE
Heath, 'tis not His judgment. To image the vengeful father bending His bow and loosing arrows of death against us is as superstitious as — as ignoring precaution and lodging at the brink of the pit.

HEATH [backing away]
Or as embracing a dead man.

[Countryside. Sounds of a river. FOE crosses, eating apple.]

FOE
A plague is armed with terrors not every man is fortified against, but to stay as my particular friend Doctor Heath stayed was like charging Death himself on his pale horse. . . What a sight: London drawn not to the life, but to the death.

[Writes.]

Not bad. Curious, in this plague no alteration appears in any vegetable or animal besides the body of man. Other things keep their integrity: Plums, pears, cherries, apples —

[Bites apple.]

Plentiful, and so sweet.

[Enter ROBERT, who sees FOE, stops.]

Come ahead, I am sound.

[ROBERT stands still.]

How do the people hereabouts? Not so bad as in the city, is it?

ROBERT
Alas, sir! All dead or sick.

[Points.]

There they are dead and the house stands open. A thief ventured in, but he paid dear: Last night they carried him to the pit. There they are dead, the man, his wife, five children. There they are shut up. See the watchman at the door? There too, all dead. We are poor, and this they call the poor man's plague.

FOE
What do you here alone?

ROBERT
Why, I am not yet visited, though my family is, and my daughter dead.

FOE
How do you mean, then, you are not visited?

ROBERT
Why, that's my house. My poor wife and sons are visited, but I do not come at them.

FOE
How can you abandon your flesh and blood?

ROBERT
I don't abandon them. I work for them and keep them from want.

FOE
Well, but how are you kept from the calamity?

ROBERT
I am a waterman, sir. There's my boat. I work in it in the day and sleep in it at night. What I get I lay down upon that stone and my Rachel comes and fetches it.

FOE
How can you get money as a waterman? Nobody goes by water these times.

ROBERT
Do you see there, five ships lying at anchor? And eight or ten riding above the chain, two by two? Those ships have their owners on board. I fetch things for them, that they may not be obliged to come on shore. 'Tis a very fine sight!

FOE
Are they safe?

ROBERT
Every tide carries bodies. I seldom step on shore here. I am come now only to give my Rachel a little money.

FOE
And how much hast thou gotten for her?

ROBERT
Four shillings. 'Tis on the plague stone. I am waiting for her. Poor woman! Her swelling is broke and I hope she will recover, but I fear the children will die, but 'tis the Lord—

[RACHEL enters, weeping as SHE exchanges look with ROBERT.]

FOE
Did she find your four shillings?

ROBERT
Rachel: Did you take the money, Rachel?

RACHEL [picking up money]
Yes.

ROBERT
How much is it?

RACHEL
Four shillings and a groat.

[Exits.]

FOE
Friend, call thy Rachel again, and give her a little more comfort from me.

ROBERT [calling]
Rachel— Thank you, sir.

FOE [holding out coin]
Well, but here 'tis.

ROBERT
Oh sir, if you would place it on the ground, sir, that I may —

[FOE puts coin on ground, backs away. ROBERT carries coin to stone, backs away as RACHEL enters.]

RACHEL
Kind sir, thank you.

ROBERT
Thank you, sir.

[RACHEL takes money, exits weeping. Exit ROBERT.]

FOE [throwing apple]
Son of a bitch.

[JUDITH, MRS. ASH, ASH DAUGHTER drag trunk on, take out silks, drape ONE ANOTHER, dance laughing in a ring.]

How it was brought over to us never was known, at least not publicly. It was rumored to have come over in a parcel of silks imported from Holland and opened in a house in Drury Lane. In that first house the first person died.

[Dancers toss silks.]

Her neighbor came to visit, then went home, gave it to her family and died.

     [Toss.]

A minister came to pray with those of the second house and immediately he got home, he died.

     [Toss.]

And so on. From that house in Drury Lane spread the plague that carried away a quarter or more of London.

     BUCKINGHAM [off]
Bring out your dead! Bring out your dead!

     [Dancers drop silks. MRS. ASH
     and ASH DAUGHTER run
     off.]

     FOE
In September the weekly bills topped ten thousand. Death raged in every corner. They died by heaps and were buried by heaps. But then the case altered. With the first chill of fall, the poison went out of the sting. Tokens dried up and went away, inflammations went down, fevers ended.

     [Sees JUDITH.]

You.

     JUDITH

You.

FOE

What's your name?

JUDITH

What's it to you?

FOE

Much. Come over here. How do you?

JUDITH [not moving]

I'm alive, I don't know why.

FOE

'Tis my fortune also, to live.

JUDITH

Why?

FOE

I don't know. I was without armor. Naked before this onslaught.

JUDITH

How can we live without armor?

FOE

We cannot live in armor. To live is to live disarmed and innocent. There is no safety. I am without armor, and inside of me—

JUDITH

Stop.

FOE
But inside of me my heart is dark, abandoned, half dead, not assured of survival.

JUDITH
Then we are fellows. But cannot light enter in?

FOE
This I have learned, that the living, they have to live.

JUDITH
My name is Judith.

FOE
Judith.

[THEY kiss.
　　JOHN SELKIRK and ESTHER SELKIRK enter. BUCKINGHAM enters opposite, pushing wagon piled with clothing, and begins to pick up silks.
　　FLASH at TYDINGS' window.]

TYDINGS
Selkirk! What news?

JOHN SELKIRK
Tydings, good news: The plague is finished!

GOOD TYDINGS [rushing upstairs]
What news?

TYDINGS
We have arrived!

[Emerges downstairs, MRS. TYDINGS and GOOD TYDINGS following.]

ESTHER SELKIRK
'Tis life to us from the grave, but alas! More Sabbath-breaking takes place than before we heard God's voice in the city.

JOHN SELKIRK
We survived, Esther. Don't make me regret it.

BUCKINGHAM [bitterly]
What an alteration!

TYDINGS
'Tis wonderful. 'Tis a dream!

[Picks up silks.]

Somebody's left a lot of property strewn about. Sir, are these your fabrics?

BUCKINGHAM
Yes, they are!

MRS. TYDINGS
Air! The sun! Have we survived?

GOOD TYDINGS
Yes, Mother, we made it through.

MRS. TYDINGS
Your father did it. He brought us through.

GOOD TYDINGS
We still living. So many dead.

FOE
It was unlooked for, extraordinary, and no account can be given of it. The plague was over.

> [Steps around BUCKINGHAM and TYDINGS tugging at silks.]

TYDINGS
That's mine!

BUCKINGHAM
Mine!

TYDINGS
Give it me, plague take you!

MRS. TYDINGS
No new medicine stopped the infection, no skill of the physicians: Human help and human skill were at an end.

ESTHER SELKIRK
Nothing could have stopped it but

> [raises forefinger]

the immediate finger of God.

> [JUDITH looks up intently.]

FOE

What do you see?

JUDITH [pointing]

Oh, I see a portent—I see it plain!

FOE

What is it?

JUDITH

There above: A dark cloud. 'Twill rain today.

[FIDDLER playing, MRS. TYDINGS and ESTHER SELKIRK dance.]

MRS. TYDINGS, ESTHER SELKIRK

Ring around a-rosy,
  Pocketful of posy,
Ashes, ashes,
  We all fall down!

[ESTHER SELKIRK falls down, kneels in prayer, ignoring BUCKINGHAM's helping hand.]

TYDINGS

'Tis a hungry city, Selkirk. I smell opportunity.

JOHN SELKIRK

My ship embarks in three days' time.

JUDITH

What if it come again?

                    FOE
If, Judith? *When.*

                GOOD TYDINGS
Mr. Foe, join the celebration! 'Tis over!

                    FOE
Over till it come again!

                [COMPANY freezes, exit one
                by one, leaving onstage FOE
                and JUDITH.]

Fire follows plague. Within nine months, from a spark struck in a baker's house in Pudding Lane, I see the city purged by a fire that burns so fiercely the citizens give up. All this

                [gestures over audience]

I see dancing in towers of flame, then lying in ashes.

                   JUDITH
Will you come to bed? Who knows what will happen?

                    FOE
But if it come again, it will end also.

                   JUDITH
Does your work never end?

                 FOE [at desk]
I'm almost finished.

                  [Writes:]

"What the agent of infection was—"

JUDITH [tiptoeing off]
Agent of infection!

FOE [writing]
"What the agent of infection was never will be known. Some say if a sick man breathes upon glass, a strong lens can make out monstrous tiny dragons. But we only know, whatever the shape of the agent, its size was no bigger than a flea.

"I can go no farther here. I shall conclude my account of this calamitous year, therefore, with a coarse but sincere stanza of my own:

A dreadful plague in London was
   In the year of sixty-five,
Which swept an hundred thousand souls
   Away – yet I alive!"

[Holds up page. As it bursts into flame and floats off, FOE eagerly follows JUDITH off.]

[END OF PLAY]

AND OTHER PLAYS AND ADAPTATIONS –

Chesterfield to His Son

A Rude Romp in One Act
Adapted from *Lord Chesterfield's Letters to His Son*

For my father

Chesterfield to His Son

CHARACTER

PHILIP STANHOPE, 4th EARL OF CHESTERFIELD, a small man, flawlessly groomed, beautifully dressed; poised if self-conscious. Seventy years old at rise, he soon revisits his prime.

SCENE AND TIME

The library of Chesterfield House, London, evening of March 16, 1769.
Armchair. Side chair. Small table. Larger one set for a meal, with carving knife, cutlery, glasses, teacups. Sword. Dictionary and other books. Map. Magnifying glass. Fan. Wigstand and wig. Hat.
On a silver salver lies a parcel of letters tied with black ribbon, a black-bordered envelope propped against it.

AT RISE, CHESTERFIELD enters, cane in one hand, ear-trumpet in the other, in HIS pockets a snuffbox, handkerchief and watch.

>CHESTERFIELD
>[raising ear-trumpet]

Thank you, John. A black-bordered letter from Dresden? Yes, I find it, thank you.

>[Inspects envelope.]

A black-bordered letter—in a lady's hand? Absurd: I know no ladies at Dresden, in mourning or out of it. Years ago! The only person I know there now is the King's Resident—my son—who seems unacquainted with ladies—or women—at all.

Lady's hand? None of the best.

>[Replacing black-bordered envelope, unties parcel, sorts through letters, opens first.]

More letters? Not in a lady's hand. But I know this elegant writing: This is *my* hand: "Master Philip Stanhope." "Philip Stanhope, Esquire" at Leipzig, Venice, Rome, Paris, Turin. John!

Hah!

– A JOURNAL OF THE PLAGUE YEAR,

[Ribbon in hand, throws off old age.]

Dear boy: I am told, sir, that having attained the age of five, you set off on your travels, beginning by Holland.

Holland is the finest of the Seven United Provinces which form the Dutch Republic. A republic is a free state without any king. I wish you favorable winds. Should you make any curious observations, be so good as to acquaint me with them. *Adieu!* In proportion as you deserve it, I shall always be, Yours.

Now that you are eight, oh, the improvements I expect! Do well at school and in time you will know more even than myself. I shall forgive you. What pleasure to be more learned than other boys! What honor! What applause! Caesar could not bear an equal at Rome. Why should you at school? *Adieu!*

Your letter pleased me, though I believe you had help. Remember you are ten years old: Write without assistance. Write as if we were conversing:

My dear papa, I spent the morning at Mr. Harte's, where I translated English into Latin, Latin into English so well that at the top of my paper he has writ *optime*. I likewise repeated a Greek verb, remembering that as everybody knows Latin I will distinguish myself more by Greek. Then I ran home like a little wild boy and played till dinnertime, when I ate like a wolf. *Adieu,* papa.

Well, sir, *this* is a good letter.

AND OTHER PLAYS AND ADAPTATIONS –

It is important to write well. It is above forty years since I wrote one word without considering whether I could not find a better. Style is but the dress of thoughts, yet however well-proportioned your person, it would be indecent to exhibit it naked: It wants adornment.

Think also of your gestures, your air and of your *e-nun-ci-a-tion*. Trust an old stager going off as you are coming on: These things form your connection with gallery and pit.

If I use words new to you, seek for them in the dictionary. For example, "connection": Noun substantive. A uniting, joining or tying together. One says of two friends, *There's a great connection between them*. Also of things that resemble each other, *They are connected*. You and I are mightily connected. There is no closer connection than that between father and son.

Translate into French:

My dear papa, You do praise me, but you make me earn those praises by working me like a galley slave. No matter, glory cannot be too dearly purchased. So thought Alexander the Great, and so thinks Philip the Little. *Adieu,* papa.

Parliament is the theatre where you will make your fortune and figure. Success there will remove any prejudice regarding your birth— will remove all objections. To that end, I propose to unite in you the scholar's knowledge with the courtier's breeding. It is therefore time you went abroad, to form your manners on those of the best companies, until you come of age and can enter the House of Commons: By residing *in* every country (you begin by Germany) you will become *of* every country. You will return no longer an Englishman, but a

European. Considering the care I take with you, you ought to be at thirteen what other boys are at sixteen.

People your age are as apt to think themselves wise enough as drunken men are to think themselves sober enough. You have no experience of the world. I will inoculate mine upon you and prevent the pockmarks of youth. Put on the armor of my experience. Let it clear your way of the thorns which scratched me and you will unite—join—*connect*—two things seldom seen in one person: the powers of youth with the caution of age. I do not so much as hint how dependent you—son of an excellent but unmarried mother—are upon me. You have neither rank nor fortune, and I shall perhaps be out of the world before you are in it. What then will you have to rely on? *Eh?* Nothing but your own merit. *Adieu.* May you continue to deserve my love! Godspeed to you and Mr. Harte!

Your friend Sir Charles Williams is returned from seeing you at Leipzig. He puffs your modesty, your vivacity, *et cetera*. If I had faith in love potions, I should suspect you had given him one. Fortunately—for you—Sir Charles also mentions a deficiency in the Graces: Scrambling at table. Overturns of glasses. Horseplay.

Horseplay? I recommend you, sir, sacrifice to the Graces! Force them to adorn all you say and do, every word, look, tone of voice, gesture. I admit the Graces are not natives of Great Britain—of Germany still less (however, while you are there, you need not say so). But they are not inexorable ladies: They may be had. If not willingly, then ravish them—for they pave the way to the heart. Aim at the heart. Women are guided by nothing else, but even with men the heart always triumphs over reason. To strike it, intrinsic merit alone will not do: You must please.

[Belts sword on, puts on hat.]

I cannot reduce this art of pleasing to rules. Perhaps *Do as you would be done by* comes closest. Reflect how a man of fashion prepossesses you, coming into company with assurance, speaking even to people he does not know, his person pretty, motions graceful, voice harmonious, something cheerful in his features — but without laughing. Then reflect what impression an awkward, slovenly, drawling stranger makes. Yet he may have merit.

The very accoutrement of a gentleman encumbers a vulgar man. When he shambles in, his sword gets between his legs, trips him. His clothes so constrain him, he seems their prisoner. Indeed he presents himself like a criminal at the bar frighted out of his wits. His very air condemns him. Bashfulness is characteristic of the English booby.

He takes the one seat where he should not sit, and drops his hat. In picking it up, he drops his cane. In recovering his cane —

[Drops hat.]

A *quarter of an hour!* before he's in order enough to sip at tea — which scalds his mouth! Spills in his breeches! If someone happens to laugh, they laugh at him, he knows it. He is slighted, grows testy, issues a challenge, *draws*.

A gentleman never suspects himself laughed at. If something malicious be said of you, conceal your anger — seem not to understand what you must resent. I always put these jackanapes out by saying, "And—?" as if the sting were still to come. "Yes, and so?"

If you cannot pretend ignorance, join in the laugh. Acknowledge the hit to be a fair one. Play the thing off in seeming good humor. Do not reply in kind: Saying a witty thing makes more enemies than anything else. People fear a wit as a woman fears a gun, which she knows will go off by itself. Any suspicion that you love somebody less than they love themselves is an insult never forgotten and never forgiven.

At dinner our bumpkin carves—scattering sauce in everyone's face—puts his spoon into every dish, eats with his knife, picks his teeth, and when he drinks—

[Sprays.]

His hands go in perpetual motion from bosom to breeches to bosom, he makes faces, whistles, scratches his head, yawns, breaks wind or blows his nose and looks in his handkerchief—making the company sick.

None of this is criminal—but does it please? The world is taken by the outside of things, and we must take the world as it is: You nor I cannot set it right.

Who has the most friends and fewest enemies is strongest. I don't mean intimate friends—no man can hope for half a dozen in his life—but friends in the common acceptation of the word: people who would rather do you good than harm (but never put yourself in your friend's power, for he may one day be your enemy).

Young people have an unguarded openness which makes them the prey of the artful. The same tricks boys tried on you for balls, bats and halfpence, men will use for other purposes. The more you know men, the less you will trust them. Your only sure guide is he who has gone all roads and can point out to you the best.

Why did *I* go any bad roads? For want of a guide. My father did not desire to advise me. This you cannot say of yours. *Adieu.* I return your letter corrected. It had few errors, but you should know them.

Will you shirk these dictates of a sermonizing father? Advice is seldom welcome — those who need it the most like it the least. Consider them rather the advice of your best — indeed your only — friend.

But do not mistake my affection for a mother's. I am your father. My care is not mere health: My object is to have you fit to live. If you should not be fit to live, I would rather you die. Affection makes me care more about the manner of your life than its length.

This thaw will undoubtedly bring me a letter from you. In it I'm glad to find that you apply yourself and reflect upon what you learn. I applaud you. Simply to repeat other people's thoughts is the talent of a parrot — at most that of a player. But make your letters more minute as to your motions and transactions and the company you keep. Trifles concerning you are not trifles to me. *Adieu.*

Your friend Sir Charles Williams is home from Germany.

He dined with me last night. While I held the seals of state I never examined a prisoner so closely. I racked him — gave him the question ordinary and extraordinary — turned the screws and — extorted not one word against you. Go on so, you will be what I despaired of: Somebody.

He says you have grown taller than I, except you still stoop. If you get up to five feet ten — five feet nine — I would settle for five feet eight! — even your square figure would please. Send me a thread your length exactly.

Sir Charles did let fall one absurd item: your thick *e-nun-ci-a-tion*. Good! God! What kind of figure will you make in company? In Parliament? Who will listen? Who will like you? Do you propose using signs in place of speech?

Oratory makes as large a share in our government as in Greece or Rome. The business of oratory is to persuade. You cannot persuade people unless you please them.

Suppose you wished Mr. Harte to give you a holiday, would you say, Give me a holiday? That would not please him. You must first speak elegantly, clearly, using proper metaphors. Tell him his goodness encourages you to ask a favor: A holiday. Give your reasons, that you have such-or-such a thing to do, place to go. Urge that as the bow is stronger for being sometimes unstrung, so the mind improves for being sometimes relaxed. And then enjoy your holiday.

I propose Demosthenes for your model. He spoke by the sea in storms to accustom himself to tumultuous public assemblies. He put stones in his mouth and opened his lips and teeth and *e-nun-ci-a-ted* distinctly enough to carry the length of my library. But he made his strongest push at the passions. They govern mankind. Strike at people's pride, love, ambition, you need not fear their reason. The roads to the heart lie through the eyes and the ears. Eloquence is the sharp end of the nail, the point you hammer in to make way for your solid parts. Charm your audience, warm it, then forcibly ravish it. *Adieu!* I tell you truly, I shall judge of your parts by your *e-nun-ci-a-tion*.

Ah: Venice sees your premier excursions into polite company? Had I the ring of Gyges which renders the wearer invisible, I would go there to reconnoiter you, myself unseen. I would take you at breakfast, listen to your unguarded conversation with Mr. Harte. Hearing your pertinent questions, judicious reflections, how I should rejoice! Then I would observe you presenting yourself to men of sense, see whether your address is respectful, yet easy — modest, yet unembarrassed — whether your speech makes you intelligible. In the evening I would follow you to the assemblies and watch if you trifled gracefully. Should people cry out, *Che garbato Cavaliere, il piccolo Stan'ope! Com'è disinvolto, spiritoso!,* I would assume my own shape and embrace you.

But if the contrary happened — If people should point — *laugh* — I would sink my disappointment and steal invisibly home again. Imagine me always present, seeing and hearing all that you do. Be assured I have eyes upon you, and will have more at Rome.

When you write — which by the way you do pretty seldom — make your letters a journal of your life: the company you keep,

— A JOURNAL OF THE PLAGUE YEAR,

acquaintances you make, what your pleasures are. Have you begun getting the diminutives in *-etta, -ina, -ettina*?

At your age, nature takes care of the body. Not so the mind. Every hour does it essential good or lasting harm. A coachman is born with organs as good as Sir Isaac Newton's, but by study Sir Isaac is as far above him as he is over his horses. The books most people read nourish the mind as whipped cream does the body — the Oriental ravings of *The Arabian Nights,* for example. Others loll and yawn and say they have no time to begin anything. The present moment is the only one we are sure of — as such the most valuable. Never put off till tomorrow what you can do today.

I know a gentleman so good a manager of his time he will not lose even the minutes which calls of nature oblige him to pass in the — necessary-house.

[Sits, tears page from book.]

In those moments he goes through the Latin poets — has with him a leaf or two from a cheap edition, reads them and sends them down

[balls up, drops page]

a sacrifice to Cloacina. Follow his example. It makes any book very present in your mind. I wish I had known these things at your age. *Adieu, Monseigneur.* I never received the letter you refer to, if you wrote it.

[Stands up.]

P.S. Yours just received: I forbid you to cut off your hair! Your headaches cannot proceed from thence, and at your age your own hair is such an ornament, a wig such a disguise, that I—I *forbid* you to cut it off!

Rome will test you, as she tests all young Englishmen. The character young men first aim at is that of *a man of pleasure*. But for what makes a man of pleasure they adopt what they are told instead of consulting their own appetites. But the glutton, the sot, the rotten whoremaster do not enjoy their pursuits: They are human sacrifices to false gods.

I am ashamed to own to you—but as it may be of use, I do own it—that the vices of my youth came from my wishing to be called a man of pleasure. I smoked, despite my aversion to tobacco, because I thought it made me look like a man. I hated drinking, yet I drank. Same as to gaming: I plunged into it—made myself solidly uneasy for thirty the best years of my life. Take warning: Let no one impose pleasures on you. Choose them for yourself.

I suggest the most exclusive evening assemblies as likeliest to give you pleasure. If breakfasts or idle parties into the *Campagna* are proposed, beg to be excused. Lay it all on me.

Englishman: "Come to breakfast tomorrow? There'll be four or five of us sauntering, illiterate English, and afterwards we'll drive out."

[Sits on armchair's edge.]

Stanhope: I am sorry, I cannot. I must stay home all morning.

[Stands.]

Englishman: "Then we'll come breakfast with you."

Stanhope: No, tomorrow morning I am engaged.

"Then the next day!"

I never go out before two.

"What the devil do you do?"

I study with Mr. Harte.

"Are you preparing to take holy orders, then?"

My father's orders I must take.

"You mind an old fellow a thousand miles off?"

If I don't mind his orders, he won't mind my allowance.

"The old prig threatens?"

He has never threatened me, but I had best not provoke him.

"Pooh! One angry letter would be the end to it!"

[Sits down, leans far back.]

You mistake my father. He always does more than he says. If I provoke him, he would never forgive me. I might beg and beg: He would be coolly immovable.

[Stands.]

"He's an old dog, then. And you mean to obey your nurse Mr. Harte? Egad, I've a nurse myself, but I haven't seen his face this week and don't care a louse if I never see it again."

Mr. Harte desires only what is for my own good. I like to be with him.

"At this rate they'll call you a good young man."

That will do me no harm.

"Tomorrow evening, then? I've some fine wine."

Tomorrow? No, tomorrow I sup at Cardinal Albani's and go on to the French Ambassador's.

"How the devil can you stand those foreigners? I'm never easy with them. I don't know why, but they make me — bashful."

Not I. I get the languages and their characters by conversing with them. Are we sent abroad to herd with our countrymen?

"And their women of fashion! I never know what to say."

At least they've done you no hurt — more than you can say of the women you do converse with.

"I'd rather keep company with my surgeon than with women of fashion."

Tastes differ.

"Yours is devilish odd, Stanhope: The morning with your nurse, evening in company, all night afraid of Old Daddy. I'm afraid there's nothing to be made of you."

[Beams upwards sublimely]

I'm afraid so, too.

"Damn these finical airs. Give me a manly English buck! Well, good night, Stanhope. You've no objection to my getting drunk? Then going to the play to gape at the lights? Then finding a whore?"

No, no, nor to your vomiting and headache tomorrow, nor to your losing your nose to your whore's pox, nor to her protector running you through the body. Good night to you, good night.

[Leers.]

Vice so shocks us at sight, I should as soon think of warning you against it as I would not to fall into the fire. Whereas virtue seduces us at sight, so charms us that excess seems impossible. But beware!

[Dropping ribbon, stands athwart it.]

Across a very fine line every virtue runs into a kindred vice. As generosity runs into profusion, the respectful goes into the abject. Economy runs into avarice. Frank becomes indiscreet. Courage, rashness. Caution, timidity. Ostentatious puritanism becomes criminal relaxation.

In manners, this line is good breeding: Beyond it is troublesome ceremony, short of it is negligence and inattention. Only good sense and attention can keep you on this line.

> [Picks up ribbon.]

Hold on to my traces. Let me guide you through the maze.

Whereas civility — the disposition to accommodate others — essentially is the same everywhere, good breeding — the manner of exerting civility — is local. To the emperor at Vienna instead of bows men drop curtsies.

> [Curtsies.]

In France nobody bows to the king nor kisses his hand, but in England, bows are made and hands are kissed.

> [While bowing:]

As to the Pope I'm not certain he doesn't offer his breech to be kissed. (Kiss whatever his etiquette requires.)

Common sense cannot tell me why these ceremonies came to be, yet it tells me to conform to the good breeding of wherever I may be. Be flexible with regard to things not wrong in themselves.

Manners are to any particular society what morals are to society in general: their cement and their security. Utility introduced manners as it did commerce: I sacrifice such a conveniency to you, you sacrifice another to me. Good manners are the currency of society. And as laws enforce good morals, so do rules punish bad manners. The man who invades your property you hang. The man whose manners offend, you banish. Between kings and subjects the implied contract is protection — obedience. Among civilized people: mutual complaisance.

Some rules always hold true. It is rude to answer yes — no, without adding sir, my lord, or madam. Rude to speak of Mr. What-d'ye-call-him or Miss Thingum. Rude to finish a story with, "I forget the rest." (Very bungling.) Rude when people speak to you to play with a dog, pick your nose, twirl your snuffbox, look around so much as to say, kiss my breech. I have seen men knocked down for less.

But not to be rude is not enough: Be civil. There is a gruff look and a civil look. Never argue with heat, though you know you are right. Wear your learning like your watch — in your pocket.

> [Pulls out watch, strikes it.]

Do not pull it out and strike it to show you have one. If someone asks the time, tell it. Do not proclaim it like the watchman. If you contradict anybody, soften it. Brutal to say, "That's not so, I know better." Rather, seem open to conviction. Say, "I beg your pardon, I believe you mistake, if I may take the liberty of contradicting you, I am not sure, I may be mistaken, but I should rather think—" *Et cetera*. Look people in the face. Not doing so implies conscious guilt. Besides, you want to see what impression your words make. I trust my eyes more than my ears: People can say what they want me to hear, but faces reveal what words conceal.

> [Shades eyes, scrutinizes house.]

Thus I guess what they are saying—even thinking—when I cannot hear a word.

Politeness is due even our inferiors. We don't compliment them, don't talk of their doing us the honor *et cetera*, but we treat them with affability. We are all made of the same clay, some of the lumps coarser, some finer. Distinctions between us arise from fortune. Victor who cleans your shoes, Lisette who washes your linen would be your equals were they as rich as you. Being poor, they must serve you. Do not add to their misfortune by reminding them of it: Endeavor to make them forget it. Use even the beggar in the street with good breeding. Consider him the object of compassion—not of insult—and refuse him with humanity.

I must warn you against laughing. A gentleman is seen to smile—even seen to laugh: Never heard. Nothing is so ill-bred as audible laughter. True wit never made anybody laugh. Wit pleases the mind, lends a—a cheerfulness to the countenance. What excites laughter is the mob's buffoonery. A man's going to sit down thinking there's a chair behind him and—

> [Falls.]

Oh, *that* sets the company a-laughing. Proof how low a thing it is, not to mention the noise it makes, the distortion of the face. Since I gained the use of my reason, nobody has heard me laugh.

Your friend Sir Charles Williams sings your praises—of your modesty especially.

Modesty is a fine quality. I am pleased that you avoid speaking of yourself. Some do so without provocation.

Impudent! Others go to work more slyly—lament being so weak they cannot see suffering without trying to succor it, see need without relieving it, cannot help speaking truth— Oh, but they are too old to change, must rub on the best they can. (Take my word, you'll meet characters so extravagant no dramatist would set them on the stage.) Never drop one word that can be construed as fishing for applause. A man who speaks little of himself but extols other people acquires love and esteem. Thus (by the bye) does modesty gratify vanity.

Modesty, then, is admirable. However, if it is possible to be too modest, you are.

Human actions have one principle: vanity—self love—the desire of applause. Where vanity is wanting, we are listless, indolent, inert when we should be *alerte, adroit, vif*. Who loves himself most is the most honest man. If you prefer, the most honest man loves himself most.

That our actions derive from self-love is a reflection much blamed, but why? I blame only mistaken vanity—taking immediate gratification for happiness. If I do a good action, am I blamable because it makes me happy? Give me virtuous actions, I will not quibble about motives. I think that next to doing a good action, the most pleasing is doing a *polite* one.

I confess (you are my confessor) I had vanity to a prodigious degree—a thirst, a rage for popularity, to make every man like me, every woman love me, even women I would not give a pinch of snuff for. *My* face, *my* figure made it an uphill game, yet often I succeeded. To vanity I owe my success in life—to manners more than to merit. But you seem indifferent to admiration, you whose face and youth entitle you to it. You withdraw, recede, shun the light, when you should advance,

[advances]

shine, *dazzle*.

This greets you to Paris, capital of good breeding and — other things. I love capitals, the seats of arts and sciences and the best companies, where human passions exert all their force, all their art in pursuing their objects. Other places are worth seeing. Capitals only are worth living at.

Let your dead books now give way to the living book of the world, of which there are so many readings. Knowledge of the world must be learned in the world: You cannot learn it by theory. Take your notions of things as you find they are, not as you read they should be. They never are what they should be.

Rather than your learning Plato by heart, I would now you fell in love with some coquette who will lead you a dance, supple you. Do not imagine you are at Paris to study Notre Dame. Oh no. *Nocturnu versate manu, versate diurna.* Turn over men by day — women by night.

[Is seen to laugh.]

By all means look at antiquities, paintings, *et cetera*. This is soon done. They are only outsides. The insides of men is your science. Chit-chat will not take you inside heads and hearts. You must search deep — pry open every man for his prevailing passion. Touch him but there, you touch him to the quick. If you cannot get at him through that avenue, try the serpentine ones: You will arrive.

When I first came into company—the rust of Cambridge on me—I made fine low bows, but when I was spoken to: *obstupuit, vox faucibus hesit.* If people whispered, I knew it was about me. If they laughed, I prayed for death—suffered like the condemned at the gallows. However: I persevered. It grew easier. I began to bow not so *outré*, to answer without stammering—until one day I was so intrepid as to go up to a fine woman and say I thought it

[fingers collar]

a warm evening. She answered—she thought so too. Gradually I joined the habit of politeness to the pretense of ease.

Do not, however, in Paris go to the English coffeehouse. *Monsieur le Chevalier*—belaced, bepowdered—accosts you and, seeing you are a stranger, offers his services. He knows a lady—a lady of position.

Well, go with him and you find a painted strumpet playing cards with sharpers dignified by titles. She receives you with delectable politeness. But how to amuse you? She never allows cards—never for above a franc. Could such small stakes amuse you? Well, you sit down and promptly win ten francs. Supper comes up, you celebrate your luck, your hostess *la marquise* commences to talk sentiment. Certain oblique ogles bid you not despair. After supper, someone suggests a hand of faro. *La marquise* exclaims in horror, but you and your new friends prevail and sit down again.

Then the operation begins. They cheat you of your money, your watch, your rings, your snuffbox, your buckles—

probably for greater security murder you. In Paris this happens every day.

I inform you I have accounts of your behavior from channels of intelligence of which I do not apprise you. *Adieu.*

Three mails lost! How provoking! Letters to and from me have worse luck than other people's. It breaks the thread of my instructions!

Sir Charles Williams — your friend — writes me there is still a hitch in your

        [whispers:]

e-nun-ci-a-tion.

Your trade is to speak well. The speaker's trade is like the shoemaker's: Who applies most does best. Remember Demosthenes. To persuade, please: Tune your voice to harmony, mark your emphases and cadences, *e-nun-ci-ate* distinctly.

Imagine if they should call you Muttering Stanhope. A nickname can undo a man. Get one and it will stick. What excites ridicule? Clumsiness. Singularity. Mimics lay hold of minute defects in manners, air,

        [mimes:]

e-nun-ci-a-tion.

A gentleman's polish extends to his diction. Do not like John Trott say to a new-married man, "Sir, I wish you joy," or to a man who loses his son, "Sir, I am sorry for your loss." No: Say it elegantly, adapting your expression to the occasion. Advance warmly to the bridegroom: "If you do justice to my attachment to you, you will judge of the joy that I feel upon this occasion better than I can express it." *Et cetera*. To the grieving man say gravely, in a low voice, "I hope you do me the justice to be convinced that I feel what you feel and shall ever be affected where you are concerned."

[Struggles for composure.]

Machiavelli said the height of ability is to unite *volto sciolto* and *pensieri stretti*—a seeming frankness with a real reserve. Be upon your guard—to put people off theirs. A man of fashion, like the chameleon, takes on every different hue. Excuse me.

[Turns away, regains composure.]

How do you pass your leisure hours? Do you attend assemblies? Little suppers? Do the women say, *Ou est donc le petit Stan'ope? Que ne vient-il?* Have you a passion for anybody? Make me your confidant.

A veteran woman of condition—past her bloom, but possibly having enjoyed some gallantries—can form a young fellow better than any advice. Amicable collisions with such rub off and smooth our rough corners. A young man's attentions flatter these women. Make one of them your friend—any married woman at Paris will do. But take care never to drop one word of her experience, for experience implies age, and the suspicion of age no woman—not she turned of eighty!—ever forgives.

They tell me *Madame de Blot* is pretty. Do you frequent *la belle Madame de Case?* Are you in love with *Madame de Berkenrode? Madame du Pain?* She's handsome still, they say, and being past the glare of youth may be more willing to listen to your story. Your hour may not yet be come, but it will come. Love is like the smallpox: You get it sooner or later. *Adieu,* my son! May you turn out what I wish! When I reflect upon the manure I've laid upon you—

[FLASH]

"If I durst!" What, Blot's virtue intimidates you? Berkenrode's respectability? Case's modesty? For shame! A gentleman dares!

He begins his approaches by a rumor of assiduities, distant, glancing attacks, attentions ever closer.

If not repulsed, he advances.

After certain steps success is infallible: Those citadels always have weak places. Every man may be had one way or another—every women almost any way. The only danger in daring is not daring to dare—then they *will* laugh.

Begin by du Pain. She is not young, her choice of lovers is not entirely hers. Vouchsafe her tender looks. Tell her, "I know my questions are troublesome, but nobody can educate me so well as you." *Et cetera.* Whisper you wish your only motive were friendship—but you cherish sentiments—desires—more tender.

The first time you say this, you'll feel a fool.

So much the better: Your avowal will ring true. Dare a second time, a third— Unless the place be already garrisoned, you will take it.

As to pleasing women, I should perhaps let you into certain. . . *arcana*.

Women, then, are only children of a larger growth. They have an entertaining tattle, sometimes wit—I never knew one who could act logically for four-and-twenty hours. Their beauty neglected, their understandings deprecated, their age increased, kindles them instantly.

Women have two passions: vanity — love. Everything they say and do gratifies their vanity or their love. Who flatters them most, pleases them best. No flattery is too high or too low or too gross for them to swallow. Nature has not yet formed the woman ugly enough to doubt flattery of her person: Every woman not hideous thinks herself handsome. If her face be shocking, she trusts her figure makes amends. If both are bad, she has graces, an air, a *je ne sais quoi* more engaging than beauty.

But the conscious beauty? Listens only to praise of her mind. Do not think I recommend abject flattery. No. No, no. But if a woman wishes to be thought handsomer or wiser than she is, her error is comfortable to herself—innocent to you.

A man trifles with a woman, humors her, plays with her as with a sprightly child, but never trusts her with serious matters—though he makes her believe he does, which is what she is proudest of: They love to dabble in business. Talk to her too deep, you confound her. Too frivolously, she resents the contempt. Talk to her as below men and above children. She adores that man who talks seriously and seems to consult her. I say, seems.

These are secrets. Keep them if you would not be torn to pieces by the whole sex. In the great world a man must be gallant to the women. *Adieu.*

A bill for ninety pounds sterling was brought me this morning. I scrupled paying because I did not see your signature. The person desired me to look again — with my magnifying glass. I did then perceive somebody's mark — your name in the smallest hand I ever saw. I paid it, though I had rather it were forged than have that signature be yours. Gentlemen write their names in large characters. Your hand is a truant schoolboy's. Your *E* and *L* — strangely zigzag. A genteel hand is more important than you think.

From hand to arms the transition is natural. The motion of the arms is the material part of dancing. Dancing — however silly — is one of those follies people are sometimes obliged to perform. I would not have you a dancer, but when you dance, dance well: Be not ridiculous though in a ridiculous act. The feet do not matter. If a man dances well from the waist up, moves his head properly, wears his hat well — he dances well.

Arms decide whether a man is genteel. A stiffness or twist in the wrist will make any man look — Your dancing master is the most important man in Europe to you, for you must dance well in order to sit, stand or walk well.

Learn to come into a room. Have him make you go out and come in presenting yourself to ministers — women — mixed companies—*et cetera*. Have him teach you every attitude the human body can be put into—every genteel attitude—to loll genteelly where you may be free, to lean gracefully where you may not. Ill-bred people sit bolt upright or else loosen their buckles and welter supinely with a smirk, a whiffling activity of the legs: strong indications of futility.

Dress has the same nature as dancing. Dress yourself as others do, plain but fine, and when once you are dressed in the morning, think no more of it but go through the day as if you had nothing on at all. *Adieu*.

Your seat in Parliament is secured. Mr. Lewis brings you in at his surest borough. Break up your little establishment and come home to me: Your game begins.

Before kings meet, ministers adjust even the armchairs so they know what to expect. We want no such distrustful preliminaries: You know my tenderness, I your affection. I shall make your stay with me useful. Not perhaps pleasant: I have my glisters to administer, to inject your youth with my experience. The smallest error will not pass but call forth a look at the time, correction later on.

I am anxious at your debut upon the great stage, for I distrust your outward air. Sir Charles Williams—*your* witness—tells me you are inattentive.

Sir Isaac Newton had a right to be inattentive from that thought his investigations required. Do you claim that indulgence? If when we meet you are absent in mind, I warn you, I will soon be absent in body.

Good! God! If you come into my room on two left legs, clothes hanging, twirling your hat, muttering, blushing, a finger in your nose? If at table you knock over my glass or hack a chicken for half an hour, slopping your sleeve in gravy? It would endanger my health! I would rise from table to escape the fever.

Think of my friend Mr. Lewis. No man better — but you have seen him. He leaves his hat in one room, his sword in another — would leave his shoes in a third if they weren't buckled to his feet. His head — hanging from a scrag neck — has received the first stroke upon the block. His arms and legs have undergone the question extraordinary upon the rack. He dances so disjointed it is grotesque. I have hinted — oh, I have hinted. Now when *my* piece is to be exhibited to the public: The Graces! The Graces! The Graces! *Adieu*.

"You inform me of a very agreeable piece of news, namely, my election to Parliament is secured." This is not elegant. "Namely?" Stiff, formal. Use "that is": "that is, my election is secured." You spell induce E N. You spell grandeur U R E. My housemaids would not make these mistakes. One false spelling can fix ridicule upon you for the rest of your life. I knew a man who spelled wholesome without the *W*. He never recovered.

Two months from now your fate will be determined — one way or the other. Spectators make allowance for youth, but they will rank you by your eloquence. Your speaking must shine. I have spoken in Parliament — with applause. There is little to it. Every assembly is mob — one never talks mere reason to the mob. Give them a few harmonious periods in a speech, they go home humming the tunes like people from the opera.

The recipe is: Take a pinch of common sense, add some application to House rules, throw obvious thoughts in a new light, stir it up with handfuls of style. Do not overvalue your audience. When I first entered the House, I felt awe. That vanished when I found not thirty could understand reason. I spoke the first time with little concern, the second time with less, the third with none at all. Yet the people look upon a fine speaker as a phenomenon. If he walks in the Park they stare at him and cry, *That is he!*

I knew a young man elected to Parliament laughed at for being seen through the keyhole speaking to himself in the glass. I could not join in that laugh. I thought him wise.

[Glances at door.]

I look forward to our meeting like a bride to her wedding night: Wishes, hopes, fears agitate and terrify me. I expect pleasure, but fear pain. *Adieu!* P.S. I forgot to give you one commission when you come over: Bring the Graces with you.

[BLACKOUT]

[LIGHTS RISE]

My dear friend: I heartily congratulate you upon the loss of your political maidenhead. I hear good accounts of your first speech. Two good judges sent me compliments, though they perceived you said neither all nor perhaps what you intended. You were stopped in your career—

[pause]

but recovered breath and finished. You are mortified without reason. I know the dreadful feeling of first standing up in that chamber. I am glad you stopped. Speaking in public is but a knack, and though one may not speak like Pitt, one may make a good figure in a second rank—

> [Makes gesture of cancellation.]

You have set out well. *Adieu.*

I have disposed of your seat advantageously. Not Parliament but courts are to be the theatres of your wars! From the beginning your education was calculated for the department of foreign affairs. I think the King—after your final polish at the court of Turin—will name you his Resident at—well, Ratisbon, or perhaps Dresden. After that? It is up to you.

A general map of courts shows the ways to be crooked, that the flowers strewn over the ground conceal pits. All the paths are slippery—every slip is dangerous. Nothing is what it appears to be.

The springs of everything at courts are ambition and avarice. They create and dissolve friendships—make enemies, reconcile them. As you know, courts are the very seats of politeness, of the highest good breeding: Were they not, those who now embrace, would stab each other. Good manners, only, interpose.

> [Dangles ribbon.]

Homer supposes Jupiter letting down a chain to the earth to connect him with mortals. So at court a chain connects the prince with the page of the backstairs. That page rules his lover, a chambermaid who in turn rules her mistress, who has influence over her lover — and on *ad infinitum*. Offend nobody at court. No one is so low that by the strange vicissitudes of human affairs he may not gain power over you. Break no link by which you climb up to the prince.

You arrive at Turin fit for the final rubbing. Here is a little art which may assist you there. I allude to that pleasing flattery delivered behind people's backs — of course in front of those who will repeat it. Praise the great men the House of Savoy has produced. Observe that nature redoubled her efforts to produce King— King— I forget his name. Wonder where it will end — shake your head, throw up your hands, ask, In the domination of all Europe?

[Is seen to laugh.]

The highest flattery? Imitation. Suppose you invite somebody to dine. Provide their favorite dish, not without saying, "I saw you enjoy this, therefore I ordered it." "I saw you like this wine." The more trifling the thing, the more flattering your attentiveness.

The Earl of Shaftesbury launched a campaign of imitation when he wished to be a favorite with Charles the Second. The King's passion was women, so my Lord kept a whore, whom he made no use of, had no occasion for. The King heard of her, asked him if it was true. He said it was, adding he had more besides, for he loved variety. At his next levee the King saw him at a distance and said, "One wouldn't think that little man to be the greatest whoremaster in England, but I assure you he is." Lord Shaftesbury saw the general smile. The King said, "This concerns you, my Lord."

"Me, Sir?"

"I said you are the greatest whoremaster in England. Is it not true?"

Replied Lord Shaftesbury, "Perhaps I am, Sir—

[bows]

—of a subject."

Receiving my letters, I imagine you say, Will he never have done? Has he not said everything over and over again?

No, no, no, no, no: I grudge no trouble which can help you.

Talking the other day with Sir Charles Williams, I expressed anxiety at your neglect of the Graces, your want of—

He interrupted me.

"That *douceur* his father is master of"—he said—"is not in his nature."

I denied it. We may improve nature, I remarked.

"What! Would you have him be perfect?"

Why not?

"Impossible!"

Then as near perfect as possible. Those who aim at the mark come closer than those who leave it to chance.

"But he has a good heart, a good head. What more would you have?"

Everything more that adorns a character: manner, air, address.

"You lay too much stress on things of little consequence."

[Reacts.]

"Well, did you ever know anybody who united luster to weight, joined a courtier's grace to a statesman's solidity?"

[Stands stiffly.]

Yes, I did: The Duke of Marlborough possessed the graces to the highest degree. His figure and manner were irresistible to man or woman. Ignorant of books—extremely knowing in men. Our greatest general, sublimest diplomat. Always cool. Never any variation in his countenance. He wound up his whole machine to please. All art—no man was ever more ambitious or avaricious.

I asked Sir Charles, What hinders my boy from becoming another Marlborough? We wagered fifty guineas. You may win them for me.

I ask again for what I have asked for before: Admit me to your fireside, converse with me in your everyday clothes, as a friend, about your private life. Tell me your allotment of the day. How does the King's Resident at Dresden pass his evenings? What houses do you frequent? Who frequents yours? Are you forming connections? Have you vowed one of those eternal passions which lasts a month? In short,

[thumps floor]

let me in!

Few fathers care for their sons. Most care more for their money. And of those who do love their sons, few know how. They hurt them by indulgence. As fathers go, it is seldom a misfortune to be fatherless. And considering the general run of sons —

You and I form the exception. Nineteen fathers in twenty — *every* mother — would have ruined you. Look at the Lewises, how they spoiled their son and now quarrel with him because the world forgets to treat him as mama and papa did.

You cannot make me these reproaches. I never loved you in that mistaken manner. Our relations are based on truth and affection, and neither of us would change our position if we could. It is plain I have no motive in whatever I say to you but love. *Adieu.*

You will have read of poor Sir Charles Williams. He remains in confinement, they say for life: incurably insane — apparently been so for years. He came ranting to me that the King of Prussia was embarked on the conquest of England, then proceeded to Court, where at first they laid his exhibitions to drink, but after he took off every stitch of his clothing and chased the King the length of the state apartments, veritably offered to mount the throne of England — they handed him into the care of the doctors. Who can say whence such frenzy comes? Poor human nature holds its reason precariously.

– A JOURNAL OF THE PLAGUE YEAR,

[Gradually resumes old age.]

I do not like the return of your fever. Have you taken out a patent on it, it lingers so? I am unwell too—weary of a life that may be called still life. I wish it were gout, the distemper of a gentleman. Rheumatism is the distemper of a coachman obliged to be out in all weathers.

The leaves wither and fall and intimate that I must follow. I shall go without reluctance, only innate self-preservation makes me spin out my thread as long as I can—

[Ribbon breaks.]

In this silly world, where the chances against happiness are so great, philosophy is necessary. At seventy, I find nothing worth desiring or fearing. Winter comes. Take care to keep warm—legs and feet especially, and lungs, and head. *Adieu*. Yours till death.

My dear friend, the outside of yours of the 4th directed in your own crabbed hand gave me more joy than the inside of any other letter ever did. However, I am alarmed—no, but concerned—at the return of your asthmatic complaint while fever persists. Chew a little rhubarb. I enclose some from my garden.

Exert your attention now to acquiring the ornamental parts of character. Many who aim to please grin ghastly grins, but you are the only person I ever knew who rejects the handsome face nature gave you. You beg to be excused, will not accept, but put on the mask of a German corporal. Change this front or nobody will knock at your door. Accustom your eyes to a certain softness, your mouth to easy smiles, your motions to that *douceur* to which—God knows why!—you are the sworn enemy. Without these Graces you are fleet of one leg, lame of the other.

> [Limps downstage.]

Without this last beautiful varnish, you will be nobody. With it—good breeding, manners, a spruce air, the glitter a young man should have: Somebody. Anything. God bless you, my dear child! And restore you to perfect health!

> [Opens black-bordered letter, drops into chair.]

Dead and—*married?*

> [Dictates, wrapping ribbon around hat.]

Mrs. Philip—Mrs. Philip Stanhope. Madam: An inflammation in my eyes obliges me to use another hand than my own to acknowledge the receipt of your letter of the

> [consults black-bordered letter]

—the 27th past. I— I—

> [angrily stands up]

I am surprised his mother objects to the manner in which you buried your husband. All any rational creature can desire is not to be buried alive, how or where must be indifferent. Pray, I bid you bring your boys here, to my house—*your* home—where I shall be glad to see you. Do not delay. Your humble servant.

Madam: I was so taken up in playing with the boys today I forgot what I meant to say: To wit, school. Let me know your pleasure as to where, I will attend to everything. Buy them everything they need, good but plain, and send me the account. From this time forward the boys shall cost you not one shilling. Your servant.

To Charles Stanhope and Philip Stanhope: I received today two the best written letters I ever saw — the one signed Charles Stanhope, the other Philip Stanhope. As for you, Charles, I do not wonder, for you will take pains. You will be a scholar, if you please. But you, Phil: You idle rogue, how came you to write so well? Do not your scrapes fill up your time?

You both say you want nothing. What grown-up people will say as much? But think and tell me what to bring you, and I will bring it.

In the meantime, God bless you! Chesterfield.

[BLACKOUT]

[END OF PLAY]

AND OTHER PLAYS AND ADAPTATIONS –

Dr. Knox and Mr. Banner

A Play in Four Acts

– A JOURNAL OF THE PLAGUE YEAR,

Dr. Knox and Mr. Banner

CAST OF CHARACTERS

DR. HENRY KNOX, an American mad-doctor at London's Bethlem Hospital, 25.

HON. FREDERICK BANNER, a saturnine painter, 30.

FLORA STURTEVANT, an American heiress, 24.

EMILY TIFFIN, also American, 32, STURTEVANT's cousin and hostess.

TOMMY, a Cockney youth, 20.

MRS. GREENE, widowed landlady to KNOX and BANNER.

SCENE AND TIME

The single scene alternately represents BANNER's studio and KNOX's laboratory on the top floors of a house in Southwark. Windows overlooking rooftops. Door. BANNER's bright studio (mainly right), strewn with props, draperies, easels and paintings, features a dais and bed. KNOX's darker laboratory (mainly left) has tables of chemical apparatus, a curtained bed and the anatomical print of a man.

ACT ONE
BANNER's studio, an evening in May, 1851.

ACT TWO
BANNER's studio and KNOX's laboratory, two nights later.

ACT THREE
Same, late afternoon, three weeks later.

ACT FOUR
KNOX's laboratory at dusk, four days later.

ACT ONE

AT RISE, the light of a May evening of 1851 fills BANNER's studio before fading away. KNOX, pacing, reads from Tennyson's *In Memoriam* (from Sections 50-51) while BANNER paints TOMMY, who in loincloth kneels on dais, arms outstretched towards empty looking-glass frame, HIS eyes following KNOX.

KNOX
Be near me when my light is low,
  When the blood creeps, and the nerves prick,
And tingle, and the heart is sick,
  And all the wheels of being slow.

Do we indeed desire the dead
  Should still be near us at our side?
Is there no baseness we would hide?
  No inner vileness that we dread?

Shall he for whose applause I strove,
  I had such reverence for his blame,
See with clear eye some hidden shame
  And I be lessen'd in his love?

BANNER
"No baseness we would hide? No inner vileness that we dread?" *Hmm!*

KNOX

An intriguing passage.

BANNER

By the flickering light of his candor I glimpse Tennyson's gargoyle features peering out.

KNOX

I never know what you mean.

BANNER

I mean death seems to have saved his friend from a worse fate.

KNOX

Oh, you're not serious, of course.

BANNER

"Inner vileness"? "Hidden shame"? They give the game away.

KNOX

In Memoriam records Tennyson's grief at the early death of Arthur Hallam. Their manly love for one another —

BANNER

— did not, I fear, exclude desire. Don't look close, he tells the ghost, lest you see.

KNOX

You mean a carnal —? Nonsense! Ridiculous! Rubbish!

BANNER

He protests too much. And Hallam engaged to marry his sister? Incestuous! Face it, he's a pouf.

[TOMMY laughs.]

Head still, Tommy.

KNOX
A *what*?

BANNER
A Mary-Jane. A son of Sodom.

KNOX
Banner, no gentleman —

BANNER
No gentleman can afford to speak truth, but surely a mad-doctor can face it?

KNOX
Friendship is founded upon truth, Tennyson's and Hallam's — for that matter, yours and mine. Friendship means the free bestowal of our purest emotions. The love of friends surpasses those kinds of love based on contract or function. That between man and woman is not so high. But to besmirch this ideal relation with intimations of Greek love —

BANNER
— deviates from the straight, high-hedged road of truth. I see: Tennyson's passion, according to your Roman *pronunciamento*, breathes of anything but Greek love. Greek love in particular does not enter into it.

KNOX
There is nothing here proscribed or forbidden. He does not cross the line.

BANNER
Knox, there are no lines in nature.

TOMMY
'Ere, talking about buggerin'?

BANNER
No, dear boy: poetry.

TOMMY
Same thing, sounds like.

BANNER
You wouldn't understand, Tommy, being without hidden or inner anything. Turn your head.

TOMMY
What am I looking at?

BANNER
You see a beautiful youth, a youth with a strange allure whom you wish to make your friend. No, don't touch yourself.

TOMMY
All I see is Dr. Knox.

KNOX
Who is he posing as?

BANNER
Narcissus.

KNOX
Good God!

BANNER [to TOMMY]
Reach to his face as to a cup you wish to lift and drink from.

KNOX

You and I have grown close, Banner, yet our feeling for each other is quite unshadowed.

BANNER

If you loved me —

KNOX

In a manly sense, I do. I am proud to affirm it.

BANNER

If you loved me, you would place no limit on your love's expression.

KNOX

Banner!

BANNER

How you act, then, contradicts what you say. Too bad, because as a scientist you might get to the root of these matters. I have hopes of science: Science deals with what it finds. In demanding proofs perhaps it refuses the spirit, but by throwing light onto darkness, it renders a chiaroscuro nearer the truth than other ways of looking.

KNOX

I hope that is so.

BANNER

Tennyson puts a lantern's light on his feelings, like a torch to straw, then runs from the resulting conflagration. Explore his verses as you would symptoms, with medical knowledge and your ability to put facts into relation, and you will find his subject to be his desire for a man.

KNOX
You miss the point completely. Tennyson mentions no such thing.

BANNER
Only disguised can his heart gain its voice. It bade him wrap his friend in his arms, kiss him, take him to bed. He resisted. Too late now. The best he can do now is to break out into the beautiful wealth of regrets and Christmases and weddings you've been reading. That is art, my dear chap. Art transforms forbidden Eros as a rosebush does manure: Makes it blossom.

KNOX
Art!

BANNER
Scorn art's alchemy at your own risk. You men of science take a substance and break it down, distill away every trace of soul or feeling, and extol the ashy remnant as the essence of the thing—the thing itself, just what it is not.

KNOX
I protest.

BANNER
Isolate what you would study, sever it from life, and you kill it. Blanch every shadow with your limelight and you enter the realms of fancy.

KNOX
Is that why you paint such murky stuff?

BANNER
But men are mixed of dark and light, and to tear one from the other distorts and destroys. The Romantics knew this, but their

breath has failed, the coals are cool and gray. I must kneel and blow them to a brighter glow.

KNOX

Why you?

BANNER

Because I am an artist. Why not make it your work too? Compound serums that bridge a man's wishes and his behavior, that animate his body with his spirit... How sad that Tennyson's loving comes out as art only, not as love. How he must regret not speaking while Hallam lived.

KNOX

I do not wish to continue—

BANNER

Only a woman, we're told, is the proper receptacle for a man's beastliness. She alone can provide the sanctioned satisfaction. Tennyson knows how he feels is not how he is supposed to feel. Hence his fear of ghosts.

KNOX

Would you have him proclaim his love?

BANNER

But that I think he has done. He might as well have got some joy of it.

[Knocks at door heard.]

Come in!

GREENE [entering]
Oh Mr. Banner, have you seen Doctor— There you are, sir. There's a lady, sir, *two* ladies, come to see you. Tried downstairs but you wasn't in.

BANNER
Ladies for Dr. Knox? Have them up, eh, Tommy?

TOMMY
Here, where are my clothes?

KNOX
Thank you, Mrs. Greene, I will receive them in my rooms. Patients?

GREENE
Oh no, sir: *ladies*.

BANNER
You are welcome to see them here. Your laboratory does reek.

KNOX
Very well. Any name, Mrs. Greene?

GREENE
They talk funny, like you. Miss Flora Sturte— Sturte— There, I can't say it, one of your American names.

KNOX
Flora Sturtevant!

GREENE
That's it! Miss Flora Sturte— Sturte—

[Exits. TOMMY gets dressed.]

KNOX
My fiancée!

BANNER
Oh?

KNOX
I knew her father was to bring her over to see the Crystal Palace, but—

BANNER
But you forgot.

KNOX
I hadn't expected her so soon.

BANNER
I'd no idea you left a fiancée across the sea!

[To TOMMY:]

Who told you to get dressed?

TOMMY
Call it a day, guv, the light's going, my flesh is coming over creepy.

BANNER
Finally paintable, my boy.

TOMMY
Not with ladies coming.

KNOX
I'm so happy. This does give me joy.

BANNER

Knox, help me with this —

[Pulls curtain, shielding dais.]

There, sir, your privacy is assured.

GREENE [showing in STURTEVANT and TIFFIN]

Miss Sturte— Sturte— there— and Miss Toff— Toff—

TIFFIN

Tiffin.

[Advances to BANNER.]

My dear, you did not exaggerate. What a beautiful head you have, Dr. Knox, like a young god's.

STURTEVANT

Henry!

KNOX

Flora!

BANNER

Thank you, Miss Tiffin.

STURTEVANT

No, Emily, this is my Henry. Henry, my cousin Emily Tiffin. Father and I are staying with her.

TIFFIN

Oh!

KNOX
Miss Tiffin. My darling Flora: In London so soon?

STURTEVANT
An excellent crossing, Henry — by fast steamer. We can stay only a moment, but I had to see you. I hope it's proper. I don't know that it is.

TIFFIN
Nor do I.

KNOX
Proper? Who cares! May I present my friend Banner? Miss Sturtevant and Miss Tiffin.

BANNER
Enchanté, Mesdemoiselles.

STURTEVANT
So this is where you live, Henry.

KNOX [stomping]
Actually mine is the floor below. But much the same.

TIFFIN
Mr. Banner, you're a painter.

BANNER
A palpable hit.

GREENE [lighting lamps]
The stink of it, Miss. I'd throw 'im out, but young men will 'ave their fads.

TIFFIN
The pungency of Art is mother's milk to me.

STURTEVANT
Emily draws.

BANNER
Then she knows the truths of this world are not aromatic. Come to that, Knox's serums poison the neighborhood. I wake up every morning expecting to see the dead walk.

GREENE
He does no dissecting here, Mr. Banner. I allow none of that on my premises.

[THEY laugh.]

That's all right, then, only having your fun with me. Your young man has his clothes on, I hope.

[Exits.]

TIFFIN
What young man is that?

KNOX
Banner's model. A respectable youth.

BANNER
Respectability is the rule of the house. Mrs. Greene is like one's mother in that regard, or better.

TIFFIN
Better?

BANNER

Whereas your mother loves you whatever you may be, Mrs. Greene admires you vastly on quarter day, but three months later all is in suspense once more. Makes one feel—respectable, somehow.

TIFFIN [admiring canvas]

What a sensitive youth! If the model is anything like— Of course you have the hands of a born painter. What is the subject? *The Annunciation?*

BANNER

Narcissus, Miss Tiffin: Narcissus reduplicated in a silvery mirror, the instant before he tries to join image with substance, desire with flesh—and drowns.

STURTEVANT

Drowns in a mirror?

TIFFIN

Do I know your work?

KNOX

He's the coming thing, Miss Tiffin.

BANNER

Only last year I showed a *Temptation of St. Anthony.* Usually he is depicted as a wizened old gentleman. Mine was Tommy here. More tempting, I thought. The dowager Duchess of Beauchamp bought it. Her piety is exemplary.

STURTEVANT

Are you a bachelor, Mr. Banner?

BANNER

Confirmed such in the ancient ceremonial of the Church of England.

STURTEVANT

And very poor?

BANNER

As a church mouse.

KNOX

Banner and I are closer than brothers. He is a help and support to me.

TIFFIN

Banner, Banner— You are not related to the Earl of Dunham?

BANNER

I have the honor of being his son.

TIFFIN

Indeed? Flora, I give you the next Earl of—

BANNER

His second son, Miss Tiffin.

TIFFIN

Oh! How hard on you.

STURTEVANT

Emily!

BANNER

Not at all, Miss Tiffin. Of course as a younger son I have my duties: Not to disgrace my family, as, incidentally, selling pictures tends to do. Also to keep a decent if seldom seen lodging, and to stand ready to assist in suitable attire at dinner parties. Otherwise I am a free man. Pursued in the marriage market? Nay, exempt: but two hundred a year. The only scandal I can raise is if I do marry on my income. I am therefore licensed to feel whatever I do feel and to do whatever I wish to do, if it lies within my means. I cannot, my dear Henry, give you the jewels your beauty deserves.

[KNOX laughs.]

TIFFIN
Be warned by an old spinster: Beware American women. Dowered with fortune enough ourselves, we can find younger sons most attractive.

STURTEVANT
Emily says if I put my mind to it I could catch a duke's son.

KNOX
What good sport. Let me help.

BANNER
Are you rich?

STURTEVANT
Oh yes, very.

TIFFIN
Flora!

STURTEVANT
Henry, how does your work progress?

BANNER
Knox never works.

KNOX
Banner never sees me work. Either I sit in my laboratory tapping a pencil against my head in hopes of jarring loose a thought, or I am off at Bedlam.

BANNER
Whose black walls shadow one's very sanity. Southwark's not a neighborhood for the fastidious, but it serves for the investigation of lunacy or beauty.

STURTEVANT
How do you think of your ideas, Mr. Banner?

BANNER
Feeling alone on earth, unable to communicate truly and intimately with even one other human being, is what inspires me. Fortunately this is the common experience, so I hope finally to have my season of popularity.

STURTEVANT [to KNOX]
We see the Exhibition tomorrow. Will you join us?

KNOX
Delighted.

TIFFIN
Perhaps Mr. Banner can come too?

BANNER
Alas, no.

STURTEVANT
I have heard so much about the Crystal Palace.

TIFFIN
I cannot wait to show it you.

STURTEVANT [picking up book]
In Memoriam. Emily's been reading it to me. Isn't it beautiful?

TIFFIN
Glorious verse!

KNOX
Exquisite. Deep feelings probed as with a scalpel.

BANNER
Rather, chloroformed and secured in a strait jacket.

STURTEVANT
To think Mr. Tennyson kept it back twelve years!

BANNER
For who knows what private delectation?

STURTEVANT
Did you see the review, before it was known whose work it was, saying it was obviously written by "the grieving widow of a soldier"?

BANNER
A natural mistake, Miss Sturtevant. The poet speaks of his dead friend with spousal love and longing.

STURTEVANT
Surely not.

TIFFIN

Hardly that!

KNOX

We were discussing the point when you came in.

BANNER

I contend he describes his feeling for Hallam in terms of Greek love.

KNOX

Banner, really!

TIFFIN

Greek love?

STURTEVANT

What is Greek love?

TIFFIN

We women, sadly, are never taught Greek. Perhaps you mean the Byronic frame of mind?

BANNER

It goes back to the *Symposium* and Plato's doctrine that we each are but half of a whole, impelled to seek out the missing complementary shape that completes us: Men, women — women, men.

STURTEVANT

I see!

BANNER

And Tennyson seems to have found his other half in Hallam.

TIFFIN
Not to take you up too severely, Mr. Banner—being unlettered in Greek—but how can one man complete another?

BANNER
It seems to have happened thus.

KNOX
But the *Symposium* specifies that men seek women.

BANNER
Don't you hear more conviction in Socrates' description of the charms of Alcibiades than in what he says about his own wife?

STURTEVANT
You are clever, Mr. Banner. And very direct.

BANNER
I speak the obfuscation of perfect candor.

TIFFIN
Obviously you have made women your study. Flora, we must be off.

STURTEVANT
Henry, I have wonderful news. Uncle Cleve wants an assistant at the Hartford Asylum for the Insane: You!

KNOX
No!

STURTEVANT
We have hoped for this from when we were children. Now we can set the date.

BANNER
Bravo!

TIFFIN
You must be overjoyed, Dr. Knox.

KNOX
Speechless. So happy.

TIFFIN
Flora, we must —

STURTEVANT
Yes, Emily. *Au revoir*, Mr. Banner.

KNOX
I'll see you down the stairs.

BANNER
Until next time. Do come back, Knox. I've no Champagne, but we'll celebrate with brandy.

[Exit KNOX, STURTEVANT and TIFFIN. TOMMY emerges.]

Ah.

TOMMY
I'll strip down again if you want.

BANNER
That will do for today. Tomorrow at eleven.

TOMMY [kissing BANNER]
Not tonight?

BANNER
Get along with you.

TOMMY
You fancy him, don't you?

BANNER
Who?

TOMMY
Dr. Knox. Be with *him* tonight, I bet.

BANNER
Knox sleeps alone on a bed of iron.

TOMMY
Cor!

BANNER
There's your shilling, guttersnipe. Back to your cesspool.

TOMMY
Tomorrow, then.

[Exits. BANNER pours brandy, studies canvas. Enter KNOX.]

KNOX
I think I see the thing lacking.

BANNER
Do you, now?

KNOX
Place a goddess above for Narcissus to worship—

BANNER
To celebrate the confraternity of eunuchs of the harem? No, thank you.

KNOX
What fun we shall have now Flora's here.

BANNER
Shall we?

KNOX
You'll come to love her even as I do.

BANNER
Think so?

KNOX
Every man must love Flora: Don't you find her charming?

BANNER
She's lovely. But on ten minutes' acquaintance I could not make out much personality. Young American women never seem to have any. Their mothers have, so one supposes there's the germ of it somewhere.

KNOX
You're not serious.

BANNER
But what need of personality has she? She's an heiress?

KNOX
Oh yes.

BANNER
And her father approves of you?

KNOX
He is reconciled.

BANNER
But she is from not to say a higher but a richer station?

KNOX
That sort of thing matters not at all in America.

BANNER
Meaning yes?

KNOX
My father is overseer at one of the Sturtevant mills.

BANNER
I see. You realize she crossed the ocean to get married?

KNOX
Ah, but if I am not yet ready — ?

BANNER
Shades of the prison house?

KNOX
Break off my researches to go home and spoon broth to the insane?

BANNER
Knox, don't be a fool. Only marriage offers true safety.

KNOX
Safety?

BANNER
Of doing your duty, of losing yourself in the racial rush to propagate. The safety, in short, of doing as others do. As a married man, you will be woven into the warp and woof of the world. You will know where you are.

KNOX
You seem never in doubt as to where you are, yet you're older than I and a bachelor still.

BANNER
You don't want to be the odd man out, lacking the domestic anchorage, rising ever more into the individual and eccentric. Besides, getting married will help, not hinder, your work.

KNOX
As it happens my particular studies may not speed with marriage.

BANNER
What *is* the mysterious subject of your research?

KNOX
You would not understand.

BANNER
I am not stupider than average. If you speak slowly, using simple words—

KNOX
Strangely enough, we touched upon it before. I hope I made my disapproval of Greek love quite clear.

BANNER
Quite.

KNOX
I am, at Bethlem Hospital, learning to differentiate among the mad. Though the taxonomy of madness be perhaps a mad pursuit, yet I have come to feel that some categories of madness can be cured.

BANNER
No!

KNOX
A striking proportion of Bedlamites — particularly those placed by good families — suffer from a particular malady. I hesitate to name it.

BANNER
You may speak frankly.

KNOX
I allude to self-pollution.

BANNER
Masturbation?

KNOX
The self-polluter may be perfectly rational until his next bout, which invariably deranges his faculties and depletes his energies until vitality itself burns low.

BANNER
Do I shock you if I agree there is no cure?

KNOX
And some suffer from a related erotic infirmity.

BANNER
Oh?

KNOX
They pursue animal congress with members of their own sex.

BANNER
Sodomites!

KNOX
Again, they can seem rational—quite able to discourse upon topics so diverse as theatre and art. But in each is lodged this gross desire to which he is the slave. Naturally their families put them away. Once in Bedlam, they lead dogs' lives, secured in strait jackets that their hands may do no mischief and fed on gruel mixed with salt-petre—a receipt the Royal Navy passed along.

BANNER
Or was it Eton?

KNOX
Some are extraordinarily attractive. One is the most beautiful youth I have ever seen: Athletic, a bright and open face, eyes that light up at sight of me. The discovery of his practices ended a brilliant career at Oxford, and now he rots in Bedlam. It is tragic.

BANNER

Can nothing be done?

KNOX

For him, possibly. Marriage to a Frenchwoman is spoken of, with the proviso that they reside at Paris and never enter Britain.

BANNER

Oh dear.

KNOX

I see such suffering and ask myself, how can Nature have so grievously misdirected her faculty of propagation?

BANNER

What is it that Sterne says? "Nature never errs, unless for pastime."

KNOX

And so I have conceived an idea. Banner, I tremble at having thought of something so tremendous.

BANNER

Tell me.

KNOX

Very well. At Harvard College I studied blood with the most eminent men in the field. Blood, Banner, is a powerful and mysterious fluid. Its composition is suggestively akin to that of sea water, but it has darker functions than just that of carrying oxygen from the lungs to the parts of the body. I think it probable that blood can carry infections, infections of unknown origin that affect men's behavior, and that one such infection causes sodomy. Banner, if a *microbe* causes that dreadful turpitude...

> BANNER

Yes?

> KNOX

If it is a disease, the cure can be found. An antidote. The end to sodomy.

> BANNER

This is superb! What do you intend to do?

> KNOX

I hope to create a serum which, swallowed and absorbed into the bloodstream, will seek out and kill the infection and allow the erotic focus to revert to the proper — that is to say, the opposite — sex.

> BANNER

How will you make this astonishing serum?

> KNOX

From healthy blood from healthy men. I am confident that healthy blood will overpower and destroy the microbes of perversion.

> BANNER

Marvelous.

> KNOX

There is, however, one problem.

> BANNER

Perhaps I can help?

KNOX

In any experiment a doctor's first patient must be himself. I must undergo this treatment myself before I test it on anybody else.

BANNER

But surely it will be without effect? You are not a sodomite?

KNOX

Quite so: A serum that cures the perversion will have no effect upon me. Therefore to test my theory I first must achieve the opposite of my goal: I must devise a serum which *induces* perversion—a serum which will actually *make* me a sodomite. There is no other ethical course. Only thus can I later be the first to swallow the reversal serum.

BANNER

Good God! The risk! What if you are permanently changed?

KNOX

If my serum works, I consider the efficacy of the reversal antidote to be virtually guaranteed.

BANNER

You would for science undertake this?

KNOX

For science and my fellow man.

BANNER

What if under the influence of your serum you fall in love with a man?

KNOX

The idea is grotesque.

BANNER
Sodomites do.

KNOX
Facts, Banner. First, how can one man sexually please another? I speak frankly because, as a doctor, I know that not only are sodomites wrong, they are mistaken. They put at naught the vital distinction between the sexes. The key to desire is not similarity but complementarity.

BANNER
I am delighted to learn that desire has a key. But what if, transmogrified into a pouf, you wish to remain one?

KNOX
That cannot happen.

BANNER
If you come to enjoy putting your arms around a man—

KNOX
Disgusting.

BANNER
Pressing your lips to his.

KNOX
Repulsive.

BANNER
Looking at and touching his member—

KNOX
Such acts go against nature, the family, the state, the church—

BANNER
No worry, then.

KNOX
But you appreciate why I hesitate to marry just yet?

BANNER
Indeed.

KNOX
I am ungodly thirsty, Banner.

BANNER [handing water]
What is your first step towards making this serum?

KNOX
I must find a man with the bad blood.

BANNER
Can you recognize sodomites?

KNOX
Yes. They have a wild look in their eyes and dark circles beneath them, nor are their eyes ever still. And their members are unusually large.

BANNER
Expert indeed. Can you not get your blood at Bedlam?

KNOX
I dare not. My research must be secret and solitary.

BANNER
And yet it might win you friends. Where will you look? Do you know their secret signs of mutual recognition? Their

chosen phrases and postures, the alleyways and squares they lurk in?

KNOX

I shall seek out scenes of the lowest debauchery.

BANNER

May I come? Or Knox, if you prefer, I can provide a sodomite to you here.

KNOX

You know one?

BANNER

Whether he will allow you to extract blood —

KNOX

I need the smallest possible quantity, and will pay.

BANNER

It is possible, then.

KNOX

Who is this — person?

BANNER

My model Tommy.

KNOX

Tommy!

BANNER

I am led to believe he is such a fiend.

KNOX

Well, he is young, robust, in good health: An excellent specimen of monster.

BANNER

I am glad he arouses your enthusiasm. Knox, forgive a delicate question: When you have imbibed your serum and your blood charges you with monstrous desire, will you — take Tommy to bed?

KNOX

To ascertain its efficacy, I must.

BANNER

Will you know what to do?

KNOX

I have studied the Attic vases at the British Museum. They are explicit. But I assure you, unnatural sexual sensations are not my object.

BANNER

Why unnatural?

KNOX

You always make me explain the most obvious things.

BANNER

But the obvious baffles me, while the unobvious is susceptible of interpretation.

KNOX

The Bible —

BANNER
Your handbook of natural science is the Bible?

KNOX
In order to procreate —

BANNER
Most lust is spent in pleasure, which surely is a higher pursuit than perpetuating our sorry race?

KNOX
Sodomy is a disease.

BANNER
What is unnatural about disease? For that matter, love —

KNOX
Banner, let me speak. Sodomy is unnatural precisely because most people wish to do things in the one way.

BANNER
Then you mean it is a taste — claret over beer, although Nature gives us both. Why is liking claret unnatural? You Americans do have the strongest bias against freedom.

KNOX
Are you quite sure you know what you are talking about? How sodomites make use of the most shameful part of the body?

BANNER
The body has shameful parts? Knox, why worry about what anyone else might endow with erotic attraction?

KNOX

If one were to carry your thought to its logical conclusion, one would say—

BANNER

To each his own.

KNOX [shaking hands]

You're tipsy. I had better say good night.

[Exits.]

BANNER

Good night, Dr. Knox. Sweet dreams.

[BLACKOUT]

[END OF ACT ONE]

ACT TWO

AT RISE, it's evening, two days later. KNOX paces laboratory, groaning.
    TOMMY, posing for BANNER, reacts to groan.

BANNER
That will be the man in the iron mask. Let's have him up, tell him the good news.

> [Stamps on floor. KNOX looks up, exits. LIGHTS GO DOWN in laboratory.]

TOMMY
Here, I know I said a pound — but me own blood. . .

BANNER
Well? How much then?

TOMMY
A guinea. Not a penny less.

BANNER
You said yourself he's a pretty-looking gentleman.

TOMMY
What if he is?

BANNER
You'll hang in the end, Tommy.

TOMMY

Not if I starve first.

BANNER

Chin up. Look more inviting and less knowing, if you please. . . All right, do as you must.

[KNOX knocks and enters.]

KNOX

Banner?

BANNER

Come in, stranger! I expected you yesterday — in pursuit of your researches.

KNOX

Miss Sturtevant and Miss Tiffin took me to the Crystal Palace for the day. With a concert in the evening.

BANNER

Was it fun?

KNOX [taking apple from bowl]

Oh yes.

BANNER

Don't eat that.

KNOX

Sorry, I should have asked —

BANNER

Eat it if you wish, but that's a Sodom apple. Ever taste one? You'll not want a second.

KNOX

Why not?

BANNER

Because despite its plump and blooming appearance — on canvas as good as any apple — it tastes of ashes.

KNOX

Hard to believe. Plump as a woman's breast.

BANNER

Good news: Tommy assures me his blood is that very fluid you seek.

TOMMY

For a guinea.

KNOX

Thank you, but I have decided not to pursue that project. I think I should leave well enough alone.

BANNER

Your thinking has progressed. Neither do I believe in tampering with Nature.

KNOX

Women, Banner, are men's salvation. They bring us in from our lost and wandering ways and turn us to account. Their weakness calls up and justifies our strength. A man who does not feel this is beyond help. Beyond mine, at any rate.

BANNER

Do I detect the charming influence of Misses Sturtevant and Tiffin? Knox, beware: Woman's dependence on our strength is a ruse. Her natural state is one of having fallen from a higher station. A countess laments her father being a duke, a landlady that she married beneath her. Every woman dwells in a state of injustice, as though when Michael with his sword drove Adam and Eve from the Garden he gave Eve a wound her daughters pass on as their leading grievance. But woman's dependence is deceptive. It gives her all the strength in the world.

[KNOX bites apple, looks disgusted.]

Told you. That apple comes from the Tree of Knowledge. All right, Tommy.

[TOMMY gets dressed.]

KNOX
Tommy, did Mr. Banner tell you what I require?

TOMMY
Yes, sir, but I don't want it known that I do services for gentlemen—

KNOX
No services are required, only half an ounce of blood.

TOMMY
Anything you like, sir—for a guinea.

BANNER
Take him away, Knox, I'm done for the day. Enjoy yourselves—and good luck.

KNOX [to TOMMY]
All right, then. Come along.

[Leads TOMMY off.]

BANNER
I wonder whether to expect upheavals from outraged Nature?

[Exits. LIGHTS GO DOWN in studio, RISE in laboratory as KNOX and TOMMY enter.]

KNOX
Have a seat.

TOMMY [at KNOX's bed]
Here?

KNOX
Fine.

TOMMY
Mr. Banner said your bed was iron. Shall I strip?

KNOX
Just your shirt.

[TOMMY removes shirt as KNOX prepares instruments and beaker.]

TOMMY
Thought you'd want me. Mr. Banner, he said you were different, but I could tell.

KNOX
What could you tell?

TOMMY
That you like me.

KNOX
All I want is your blood.

TOMMY
Why *my* blood?

KNOX
Because you sleep with men.

TOMMY
When I can.

KNOX
That makes it a suitable basis for my serum—a serum which I hope will infect me with the same propensity.

TOMMY
Don't need magic for that.

KNOX
By reversing the procedure—by starting with blood from a normal man—I will be able to reverse the effect and cure you of your wretched condition.

TOMMY
I'll be cured when I'm dead. That's the cure.

KNOX
Close your eyes.

TOMMY
Here now, those look sharp.

KNOX
The better not to hurt. I mean to cup your temples and your chest, take a few drops from each. There will be no pain. Lie back.

[TOMMY lies back. KNOX punctures HIS temples and chest, TOMMY gasping at each stab.]

TOMMY
You have a nice touch, Doctor Knox.

KNOX
Do you feel anything?

TOMMY [spreading legs]
What do you think?

KNOX
No pain, surely?

[TOMMY gasps, seems faint, closes HIS eyes.]

KNOX
Tommy? Tommy?

[Touches TOMMY's chest. No response. Caresses HIM. TOMMY opens eyes, smiles, reaches up.]

TOMMY
Mmm. Give us a kiss.

KNOX
I have what I want from you, thank you.

[Collects blood in beaker, removes implements.]

TOMMY
Don't be ashamed.

KNOX
You were very good.

TOMMY [sitting up]
I can be better.

[Falls back.]

Here —

KNOX
Lightheaded?

TOMMY
Woozy.

KNOX
To be expected. Rest a bit.

[Prepares serum at table.]

TOMMY
What are you doing?

KNOX
Your blood I put in this beaker. Heat it. Dissolve salts, add a mineral preparation. Dilute it. Precipitate it. Stir it so.

> [Beaker steams. KNOX jumps back, then advances, sniffs it.]

TOMMY
Hocus pocus.

KNOX
Now it is ready.

TOMMY
I don't like the look of it.

KNOX
Has the bouquet of molten metal.

> [Drains beaker, staggers, collapses gagging.]

TOMMY
Spit it out! Spit it out!

KNOX
Oh God! I feel it working.

> [Staring at TOMMY, undergoes a profound change.]

My body rises in gross revolt.

TOMMY
What? What is it doing to you?

KNOX
Oh God! I don't want to want this, but the engine of wrong desire engages.

[Grabs, kisses TOMMY, who responds. Arms flailing, KNOX breaks away, shoves TOMMY to floor.]

Off me, bugger!

TOMMY

You want me.

KNOX

I do not want you. I wish to help you, to free you from the thralldom of forbidden Eros, to offer myself up on the altar of science —

[Knocks heard at door, and voices. In panic KNOX pulls bed curtains, hiding TOMMY.]

GREENE [entering]

I have the key. Doctor Knox? Your lady's here to see you.

STURTEVANT [entering]

Henry?

KNOX

Oh God Flora!

GREENE

Came by herself, but I have my knitting, all's right and proper.

STURTEVANT

Henry, what's wrong? Why are you agitated?

KNOX
I'm delighted to see you, Flora. Always. But I was working.

STURTEVANT
Forgive my interrupting. I love seeing you in your laboratory concocting your marvels. But Henry, your work has kept us apart, too, for too many years.

KNOX
What do you mean?

STURTEVANT
I have something to ask of you. A favor I would not dare mention except that we have been close for so long.

KNOX
Since we were children.

STURTEVANT
Playing house on the lawn, you my husband and I your wife — save when I was *your* husband and you *my* wife.

KNOX
Flora, you're not asking me to release you?

STURTEVANT
Henry, let's elope! Today!

KNOX
Your father —

STURTEVANT
Father won't mind, not really. I want to be yours, Henry, irrevocably yours.

GREENE
A wedding! I'll break out me best for the breakfast, with a bit of lace the like you've never seen—

KNOX
Yes— No—

STURTEVANT
Waiting makes me afraid, Henry. Don't you see, everything will adjust to us if only we take the initiative?

GREENE
Give him a kiss, I can't see a thing.

KNOX
But marriage is a state I am not worthy of, Flora!

GREENE
Reminds me of my Jerry. Married beneath meself, of course, but when you're young, love's all you care about.

KNOX
Flora, we must talk about this. There is much we must discuss.

STURTEVANT
I came here to talk.

KNOX
Tomorrow, tomorrow. I am engaged, Flora—at work.

STURTEVANT
You should have said so.

KNOX
We will discuss everything—tomorrow.

STURTEVANT
You are not very ardent.

GREENE
After her, Doctor, let her know what you want!

KNOX
When a man's busy at his profession, it is not a woman he wants.

STURTEVANT
Of course. Say no more, I quite understand.

[Exits.]

GREENE
Here! Darlin', wait for me!

[Exits. TOMMY emerges.]

TOMMY
I'll go along now. You have my blood money?

[KNOX holds out coin, holding it over HIS head as TOMMY reaches.]

KNOX
Haven't earned it yet.

TOMMY
Your blood's up now, is it?

[Kisses KNOX's face, moves down HIS body as KNOX's

[arms descend. Confused, TOMMY looks up from HIS groin. KNOX drops coin, turns away.]

Doctor? Are you all right?

KNOX

I'm fine, you unspeakable bugger! Get out or I will remand you for theft!

TOMMY

I'm taking nothing except my fee.

[Exits. KNOX leans head on anatomical print.]

KNOX

Oh God. Grinding at me in utter confidence, sure he had me, but— I couldn't. I primed myself for degradation. Panted for the sensual riot of it! But—I couldn't!

[BANNER knocks, enters.]

BANNER

Knox? Tommy told me.

KNOX

Failure!

BANNER

Tommy thought that, even if your instrument was blunted, the change in your demeanor was marked. He says you swallowed and on a sudden began to dote.

KNOX
To plot my own moral failure—and to fail—makes me the nullity of a nullity.

BANNER
You are an idealist. I knew Tommy wouldn't do. You need a subject more from your own world, closer to your own class.

KNOX
Another man's helplessness is terribly exciting. When he lay faint in my bed, I wanted to feast on his nakedness.

BANNER
You cannot cancel your innate decency. It is laughable to see you try.

KNOX
I have made myself a monster in the shape of a man.

BANNER
Nonsense, you're what you were before, a man in the shape of a man. These things happen. Put your serum to another, sterner test, Knox: Give it to me.

KNOX
To *you?*

BANNER
Give me your Greek love serum. Could not Tommy's blood being its source have made relations with him somehow impossible?

KNOX
Perhaps. Whereas you, a subject virgin as myself. . . You would do this?

BANNER
Yes, Knox, as your friend, I would.

KNOX
You are brave. All right, then. I have a dose ready.

BANNER
Give it me.

[After brief preparation, KNOX pours glassful from steaming beaker.]

KNOX
The taste is not pleasant. Something metallic to the flavor.

BANNER
They say you can summon the devil from a beaker of blood.

KNOX [handing glass]
Take it in a gulp.

BANNER [holding glass]
I feel it working!

KNOX
But you haven't—

[BANNER drinks with a flourish.]

You will feel a new sensation. A novel lust.

[BANNER hands glass back, looks around as if awakened in

                    unfamiliar surroundings,
                    touches HIMSELF.]

                        BANNER
Knox.

                         KNOX
Does your blood thump?

                        BANNER
Like cannon.

                         KNOX
Do images of weird desires crowd up?

                        BANNER
Knox, shut up.

                    [Embraces trembling KNOX.]

Why are you shaking? It's only I. I want you.

                    [Kisses KNOX.]

                         KNOX
Ohh.

                        BANNER
You like that?

                         KNOX
Oh Frederick. Fred.

                        BANNER
Henry.

[After more kisses KNOX pulls away.]

What is it?

KNOX

Fred, everything makes sense at last: I love you. I love you!

[Laughs.]

BANNER

What's funny?

KNOX

My serum. It's not a failure: It's a success! A success!

[THEY resume kissing.]

[BLACKOUT]

[END OF ACT TWO]

ACT THREE

AT RISE, a late afternoon, three weeks later. KNOX, BANNER, STURTEVANT and TIFFIN enter BANNER's studio.

TIFFIN
Going over the Crystal Palace makes for such a good day's work.

STURTEVANT
But how many times can one visit?

TIFFIN
The Queen's been twenty times.

BANNER
Acres of machinery bore you, Miss Sturtevant?

KNOX
A window into Britain's infernal industrial heart, crassly pumping money. Ladies prefer the embroidery exhibits.

STURTEVANT
Oh no, I love the iron and steel as much as Father does — spindles and axles and wheels and rods grinding merrily away. Reminds me of home.

TIFFIN

There is something brutal—not quite nice—about seeing their workings exposed.

BANNER

The nude musculature of steam engines, eh, Knox?

KNOX

Mechanical organisms, doing everything but reproduce themselves. Man's future lies in thus gaining power over Nature.

BANNER

Not over himself? Does he not tend to lose self discipline even as he subdues Nature?

STURTEVANT

I hope Father did not embarrass you, peering down the smokestacks and tapping the gauges. When he actually rolled up his shirt sleeves to stoke the model steamer—

TIFFIN

The Greek Court came as a refreshment.

[BANNER and KNOX laugh.]

There's your embroidery, Dr. Knox: To look up inside the Crystal Palace and see nothing between oneself and the clouds but glass in frames of iron filigree, a veritable fairy castle, and then to greet your *Narcissus* as an old friend...

STURTEVANT

Very pretty, Emily, but you forget the world is not a *bonbon* wrapped in frills and furbelows. The world must be taken for what it is and faced head on.

TIFFIN
Child! You have taken to speaking in ciphers, my dear.

BANNER
American women tend to after they arrive here.

TIFFIN
Why is that?

BANNER
Away from home they look at themselves against a new background and— Well, some are more themselves than ever: "In Terre Haute we wear our hats so." "Oh you never see that in Terre Haute." But others are open, absorbent, wide-eyed, deep breathing, alive in a world new to them. Altogether attractive.

STURTEVANT
You are perceptive, Mr. Banner. For weeks I've been feeling no longer tied to the dreams of the young girl I was across the ocean.

KNOX
Flora!

STURTEVANT
For you and me, Henry, Olde England is the New World.

TIFFIN
Narcissus shines amongst the other commissions, Mr. Banner.

BANNER
Think so? Despite his unresemblance to Prince Albert? Placed as he is between a sober Albertian Bacchus and a bearded Albertian Ganymede?

KNOX
It's the best picture there, besides being the only one free of royal flattery. Why cannot everyone see that?

STURTEVANT
You have one faithful supporter, Mr. Banner.

TIFFIN
Two, Emily. Nor would I be surprised if Mr. Sturtevant were to buy it in for his collection.

STURTEVANT
Father did stand before it for a long time.

BANNER
Snorting the while. An intelligent man, I'm afraid.

TIFFIN
"Afraid"?

BANNER
He will have seen my *Narcissus* not as a failed portrait of Prince Albert but—

STURTEVANT
But what, Mr. Banner?

BANNER
My sincere conception of the ideal Platonic romance.

TIFFIN
I don't understand.

BANNER
Knox, come up: We shall demonstrate.

> [Jumps onto dais with KNOX, pulls curtain cord to shield them.]

KNOX
God, Fred, I've been wanting you all day.

BANNER
Have you?

KNOX
A kiss.

BANNER
One.

> [Kisses KNOX.]

KNOX
Another. Let them wait.

BANNER
Don't be greedy.

> [Loosens THEIR shirts, posing KNOX as Narcissus, HIMSELF as mirror image. Opens curtain.]

STURTEVANT and TIFFIN
Oh! Oh!

BANNER
Observe, ladies, Narcissus is entranced by what we know to be his reflection but which he believes — and hopes! — is another man. Narcissus thus is romantic —

TIFFIN
Surely in the wrong way, Mr. Banner.

BANNER
— and a figure of complete love.

TIFFIN
But of the wrong kind, Mr. Banner.

BANNER
A lonely figure deprived of a Miss Tiffin or Miss Sturtevant, but whose loving heart insists upon an object nonetheless.

TIFFIN
We want stories, Mr. Banner: Romances and dreams. Nothing so obscure as this, or so solid.

[To STURTEVANT:]

Your father wouldn't want *this*.

STURTEVANT
I think it has its own beauty.

BANNER
I hope Mr. Sturtevant approves of my next subject, Miss Tiffin. It comes from the Old Testament.

TIFFIN
Not entirely reassuring, Mr. Banner.

[BANNER closes curtain, gives KNOX a shield, pulls tapestry behind, poses at KNOX's shoulder.]

BANNER
Incidentally, Henry, how will you solve your engagement? Have you set the date?

KNOX
I don't want to marry. I want to stay with you.

BANNER
Then I'll solve your problem.

KNOX
How?

BANNER
I'll marry her myself.

[Opens curtain.]

STURTEVANT
Oh!

BANNER
Guess.

STURTEVANT
Cain and Able?

BANNER
No.

TIFFIN
Sodom and Gomorrah?

STURTEVANT
Those were cities, Emily.

TIFFIN
Of fire and of brimstone.

BANNER
Over in the shady side of the Garden. But indeed, Miss Tiffin, we are a byword of sodomical love: I give you David and Jonathan.

TIFFIN
Oh!

STURTEVANT
What do sodomites *do?*

TIFFIN
No one knows, Flora. And which one are you, Dr. Knox? You look so unhappy.

BANNER
Poor Jonathan. He so loved David. But David. . . David saw Bathsheba.

[Descends dais, arms held out towards STURTEVANT.]

TIFFIN
Mr. Sturtevant would much prefer a wedding scene to this.

STURTEVANT

Emily!

TIFFIN

Give us the wedding at Cana, if you please, Mr. Banner.

BANNER

By all means, Miss Tiffin. One beheading coming up.

[Bounds onto dais, closes curtain.]

KNOX

She said *wedding,* not *beheading.*

BANNER

Inspiration!

[Kneels KNOX at improvised block, dons hooded cloak, leans on sword.]

STURTEVANT

I beg you not to intrude, Emily.

TIFFIN

Wait for him to set the date and you will find yourself an old maid. Marriage is not a matter of drift. He puts it off and puts it off.

BANNER [putting head through curtain]

Ah but Miss Tiffin, as courtship is comedy and marriage tragedy, why hurry them?

KNOX [to BANNER]

What did she say?

BANNER

Nothing.

TIFFIN

Mr. Banner is a cynic.

STURTEVANT

Mr. Banner is disillusioned.

TIFFIN

Beware, child, the glamour of disillusionment.

STURTEVANT

What do sodomites *do*?

TIFFIN

Stop saying that word.

BANNER [to KNOX]

Now don't lose your head.

[Opens curtain.]

Ladies, I give you my bid for Mr. Sturtevant's favor and purse: King Charles the First.

TIFFIN

Oh Flora, look. Now this is impressive, Mr. Banner.

BANNER

Imagine the dreary winter morn, the cold stone block, the blazing eager sword. And the mob chants: "The king is dead, long live the middle classes."

TIFFIN

The middle classes?

BANNER

Before he stepped outdoors the king put on a woolen waistcoat that, he said, the crowd might not mistake his shivering from cold for fear. That concern for what the mob thinks: To Englishmen, a sacred moment.

TIFFIN

Fortunately his art is sounder than his thinking. Your father would like this picture.

BANNER [indicating KNOX]

And should Mr. Sturtevant wish a likeness to Prince Albert—

STURTEVANT

Henry, do you like Mr. Banner's clever talk?

BANNER

Oh, I'm the clever talker with shocking views. It is expected of me. I quip and Henry does.

STURTEVANT

What do you do, Henry? You do look doomed.

[KNOX rises, staring at BANNER.]

Can you tell me, Mr. Banner? I know something is going on. What does Henry do?

TIFFIN

Come away, my dear.

STURTEVANT

But Emily —

TIFFIN

You must take me home. I feel distinctly if only slightly unwell.

STURTEVANT [opening purse]

How much to paint your scene, Mr. Banner?

BANNER

A commission? Are you serious?

STURTEVANT

How much?

BANNER

Fifty guineas?

STURTEVANT

Done.

TIFFIN

Flora!

STURTEVANT

Half in advance.

[Counts out gold to BANNER.]

Come, Emily, I'm ready.

TIFFIN
Mr. Banner, one word of advice.

BANNER
Concerning background colors, perhaps?

TIFFIN
The freedom of your conversation does not disturb me. I am an American, and you are noble as well as an artist. But others may be apt to misinterpret. If you would safeguard your reputation, I suggest you curb your tongue.

BANNER
Poor tongue, always flapping for its freedom, always firmly tethered.

TIFFIN
We will see ourselves out.

KNOX
Flora—

STURTEVANT
I must take her home, Henry.

[Exits with TIFFIN.]

BANNER
Gold guineas, Henry! Champagne! Summon Mrs. Greene! Tell her what Champagne is and where she may procure some!

KNOX
At last flippancy gives way.

BANNER
I only worry that they will see the finished picture, realize I described it truly, and feel less like intimates of the Stuarts than butts of the artist.

KNOX
The satirist's risk, I should have thought.

BANNER
Poor Miss Tiffin.

KNOX
That King Charles' head still moves the colonial heart?

BANNER
When facts of life make themselves manifest, Miss Tiffin feels distinctly unwell.

KNOX
Fred: How could you have told them that?

BANNER
What?

KNOX
How? And to joke about marrying Flora?

BANNER
Tell them what?

KNOX
You told them in so many words about us.

BANNER
I spoke the truth. Naturally they didn't believe it.

KNOX

If they had?

BANNER

But they didn't. No idea what I was talking about. I prattled, they giggled.

KNOX

A dangerous game.

BANNER

Besides, you *are* a sodomite.

KNOX

And what are you?

BANNER

Ah, but I am what you made me. Remember?

KNOX

Did I?

BANNER

I am your creation, Dr. Frankenstein. But having rendered my services to science, I do now wish to go back.

KNOX

Go back?

BANNER

I want the antidote. The time has come for me to give up this unnatural state.

KNOX

I know what you want.

[Embraces BANNER, who is unresponsive.]

BANNER

You have prepared the antidote?

KNOX

We'll talk about that later.

BANNER

Do we not risk making it less likely to work the more we—?

KNOX

Later!

BANNER

Shouldn't we abstain?

KNOX

Now I know you're joking.

BANNER [resisting]

Henry.

KNOX

You are aggravating. Talk, talk, talk, when it's time to—

BANNER

We discussed this, remember? What if the serum went to your head and changed what you think you want?

KNOX

Fred, I assure you: The reversal serum is ready, compounded from the blood of a normal man.

BANNER
Who?

KNOX
As it happens, Mr. Sturtevant has supported my unspecified scientific research by donating a half ounce of his blood. The antidote is bottled in my laboratory.

BANNER
Get it, then. Later we shall ascertain the result in an establishment I know in St. John's Wood.

KNOX
A brothel? Why is grossness required?

BANNER
I thought grossness was the point of it, the fun of it? It's been fun, hasn't it?

KNOX
So why end it?

BANNER
I want to be comfortable and normal again.

KNOX
Aren't things good as they are? I never before felt myself so undivided and strong. And to have found you! Fred, I want to spend my life with you. I love you.

BANNER
Love in a bottle. I don't hold you responsible for what you say. Do you realize the power your serum could give you?

                    KNOX

I'm serious.

                    BANNER

You could unman any army, or seduce anyone you happen to want, success guaranteed. But if reversal's the point — giving you the power to undo the misery of untold thousands of sodomites — why wait another minute?

                    KNOX

I'll do the reversal. But not yet. Not yet.

                    BANNER

Either marry Flora and be done with it — or let her go.

                    KNOX

Then I shall let her go. Poor Flora!

                    BANNER

She will survive.

                    KNOX

But we can go on.

                    BANNER

Henry, my conviction is that notwithstanding your serum, you are a sodomite. It is your natural state.

                    KNOX

Why did I invent the serum, then?

                    BANNER

As the long way round to what you really want. A way of indulging your impulses without hating yourself. Of creating a chemical imperative to excuse the most debauched behavior. An idea only a sodomite could have conceived.

                    KNOX

Your point is moot. We both drank it. And I love you.

                [Kisses BANNER.]

                  BANNER

Let me up.

                    KNOX

No.

                  BANNER

Let me up, I tell you.

                    KNOX

Kiss me, Fred. Kiss me.

                  [THEY kiss.]

                    KNOX

Ah, you mystify me. Why do you play at being cruel? Again.

                [THEY kiss.]

I never loved anyone but you. Do you love me?

                  BANNER

I love *you*? You must be insane, Knox. We had fun. Don't spoil it.

                    KNOX

I thought—

BANNER

You think too much. I do not wish to form with you some left-handed, perverted replica of what our mothers and fathers are. You insult me when you say you love me, take me to be less than a man. I will not be despised.

KNOX

I speak only what is in my heart.

BANNER

Who would be a pouf when normality is but a quaff away?

KNOX [touching BANNER]

You claim your heart is closed — but another organ makes plain its liking for me.

BANNER

That comes of meddling with Nature. Stop that!

[Knocks at door that BANNER and KNOX don't hear.]

It's over! Get off me!

GREENE [entering]

Didn't see them go out, but —

[STURTEVANT enters. TIFFIN follows, instantly turns around.]

STURTEVANT

Are you — playing?

KNOX

Flora!

TIFFIN

I said we ought not to burst in. They are bathing. Let us retire while they dress.

[KNOX and BANNER dress.]

KNOX

What's the matter? Are you worse, Miss Tiffin?

TIFFIN

The open air was what I needed, but Flora insisted—

[Low:]

I hope it is not my fault. I remonstrated with her as to what is due her fiancé and she said she had to ascertain your feelings. I fear she is hysterical. Have you any salts?

KNOX

I do have, downstairs.

BANNER

While you are at it, get me that decoction you mentioned.

KNOX

All right, Fred.

TIFFIN

We also will accept a thimbleful.

STURTEVANT [rising]

Too late, Henry. Emily, take me home.

[Collapses into BANNER's arms.]

BANNER

Miss Sturtevant!

KNOX

Sit her down, she must rest.

[KNOX exits and, LIGHTS RISING in laboratory and FALLING in studio, enters laboratory, nicks wrist with knife and prepares serum from HIS blood.]

TIFFIN

What a mess. Your father will hate me, Flora, think me irresponsible.

STURTEVANT

But I am fine, Emily.

KNOX

Antidote, dear Fred? But of course! Drink this made of my own blood. Such a low trick. Makes a double dose of serum for you. You'll pine away for unrequited love of me while I take the true antidote and reverse my perversion.

[Holds steaming beaker aloft.]

Here, precipitated in all its potency, Tommy's essence, preserved and transmitted through me, ready to turn any man into a lover of his own kind.

[Stirs beaker.]

Poor Fred, condemned to a hole-and-corner existence, a charade never ending as bitterness turns that handsome face into a caustic mask. Oh you evil Dr. Knox. But you have been hurt and are entitled to redress your wrongs.

[Setting beaker aside, unlocks cabinet and takes out flagon.]

Reversal? Break the chains of wrong desire? The work of a moment — for me, Fred, but not for you. Here is the true antidote, the reverser of perversions, which will enable me to marry Flora and take my place among men.

[Raises flagon, pours glass.]

But I drink to you, Fred. Yes, you I toast with this living vintage. May you thrive as a son of Sodom.

[Drinks.]

Pah. And Flora, I toast my coming duty to you.

[Drinks again.]

I feel my veins fill with resolve, medicine washing the poison away and feeding every normal impulse. I want what I am not, in the shape thank God of a woman: A woman.

[Laughing, tears anatomical print off wall.]

I'm free from the nightmare of longing for a man. Poor Fred —

[BANNER enters.]

— A JOURNAL OF THE PLAGUE YEAR,

BANNER

Henry?

KNOX

Good, I was just coming.

BANNER

You took your time.

KNOX [offering beaker]

Drink: This will restore you.

BANNER

Not you?

KNOX

I took my dose already. I told you, a doctor's first patient must be himself.

BANNER

And the effect?

KNOX

It works as expected: You repel me utterly. Go ahead, drink up. You may feel a moment's nausea, but if you close your eyes and imagine the charms of the female form, you will feel a prick of excitement. It will restore you to a more ardent lover of women than perhaps you were originally.

[Throwing arm around KNOX, BANNER drinks.]

BANNER

Bitter.

KNOX

Ah, but think of Flora's waist—and her bosom.

BANNER

I'll take your word for it. She's upset, and so's Miss Tiffin.

KNOX

Oh?

BANNER

But they appear not to have understood anything.

KNOX

Of course not.

BANNER

I think it an amorous upset. And I think I can cure two at one blow: Henry, I want to marry her.

KNOX

Flora, my dear chap, is mine. If you care to enter the lists, be my guest. I am not afraid of competing with you.

BANNER

We will remain brothers in devotion to her.

[Knock at door. TIFFIN and STURTEVANT enter.]

TIFFIN

Dr. Knox, did you forget about our little draught? Mr. Banner, don't tell me you finished it?

KNOX

Not at all, Miss Tiffin. Allow me.

— A JOURNAL OF THE PLAGUE YEAR,

[Pours brandy.]

This will pick you up.

STURTEVANT [refusing]

I am much better.

TIFFIN [accepting]

Thank you.

[BANNER grabs KNOX's wrist, exposes wound.]

BANNER

Knox, what's that?

KNOX

Nothing. An accident. I forgot to bandage it.

BANNER [dashing TIFFIN's glass to floor]

Don't drink that!

[To KNOX:]

How dare you?

TIFFIN

So delicious, too.

KNOX

It's only brandy. If you will permit me.

[Pours more brandy.]

For you especially, Fred: It toughens the blood.

BANNER
No thanks, your other elixir did that.

KNOX
Did it?

BANNER [admiring STURTEVANT]
Better than I dreamed possible.

[Taps at door. TOMMY enters.
KNOX recoils.]

TOMMY
Hello, Doctor.

KNOX
Yes? Looking for Mr. Banner?

TOMMY
No, sir.

BANNER
What is it, Tommy?

TOMMY
Wanted Dr. Knox.

BANNER
Glad you're here. I meant to let you know I'll not need you in future.

TOMMY
No, sir?

                    BANNER

No.

                    KNOX [to TOMMY]

We're busy here, if you would —

                    TIFFIN

But surely this is Narcissus, stepped down from his wall? Tell us, young man, how does it feel to know you will live on forever in oils?

                    TOMMY

Forever, and can't eat today.

                    KNOX

Tommy, we are occupied, if you —

                    TOMMY

Come closer, Doctor, I dare not speak loud.

                    KNOX

I'll come no closer.

                    TOMMY

Here, what's going on? Everybody's acting strange-like. Didn't know anyone was with you, else I'd not have —

                    KNOX

Banner, you'll go with Tommy, won't you? For a guinea he'll do what you like, and I know you like what he'll do.

                    BANNER

What are you babbling, Knox? Tommy, I have done with you.

TOMMY
Doctor, I hoped that you and I, letting bygones be bygones —

KNOX
Do you need money? Go away.

[TOMMY exits.]

TIFFIN
Are you better, dear? We were fortunate to have a medical man at such a crisis.

STURTEVANT
I'm fine.

KNOX
Flora, you must rest.

STURTEVANT
And we must talk, Henry.

TIFFIN
Oh dear. Then I must stay, when they expect me at home.

KNOX
Leave her here, Miss Tiffin. I will see her home when she has rested. I am sure Mr. Banner will attend you to your carriage.

BANNER
Gladly.

TIFFIN
Flora, would that be all right?

STURTEVANT
Go on, Emily. You leave me in good hands.

TIFFIN
I'll send my carriage back, my dear.

[To BANNER:]

You have the manners of a lord, Mr. Banner, however distant from the title. Don't excite her, Doctor.

KNOX
Of course not.

TIFFIN [embracing STURTEVANT]
Such ardor, my darling! I am so fond of you.

[Exits with BANNER.]

KNOX
It's not so comfortable as upstairs, but—

STURTEVANT
Don't fuss, Henry. I'm very well here. I welcome the chance to talk. You have been acting so strangely.

KNOX
I am not aware that my behavior invites your scrutiny, Flora—darling.

STURTEVANT
Please play me for the fool no longer. I can't bear it. What were you doing to Mr. Banner in bed?

KNOX

Flora, did you think—? Decency forbids you even to know of such matters!

STURTEVANT

Such matters as *what?* Henry, are you a sodomite?

KNOX

You can't know your meaning.

STURTEVANT

I saw—

KNOX

Certainly not. I can prescribe for what ails you, Flora: Not a draught or a drug, but an old-fashioned remedy: You need a man. A husband. I have kept you waiting too long.

STURTEVANT

If only you knew how I wanted you.

KNOX

And here I am.

STURTEVANT

Not any more. Don't mock me, Henry. I was prepared to sacrifice anything to marry you, but little as I know about marriage, it's not possible now. I don't want a—

KNOX

I am not—one of them. I'm not.

STURTEVANT

We are too old and have known each other for too long to live by lies. I am out of love with you. I realized it today. I'm sorry.

KNOX
You love Banner? Is that it? Quick work, Flora.

STURTEVANT
I must go now. I'll find a hansom cab on the street—

KNOX [grabbing HER]
Take back what you said.

STURTEVANT
Henry! You scare me.

KNOX
What are you afraid of? Are you not as safe closeted with a sodomite as with your own Emily?

STURTEVANT
Henry!

KNOX
Take it back about me, Flora, or you force me to prove myself a man.

STURTEVANT
Let me go.

KNOX
By God, you force me to prove it—

STURTEVANT
Henry, don't do this. Please! No, no, stop it!

[KNOX sweeps table clear and forces STURTEVANT onto it, pushing up HER dress and

> petticoats and opening HIS
> pants.]

KNOX

I will brand you mine, spit you on my manhood. Our wedding day is come at last.

STURTEVANT

Don't! No!

> [KNOX thrusts, but fails to
> penetrate HER. HER screams
> stop, replaced by an anguished
> catching laugh.]

KNOX

Stop. Stop or I swear I will kill you.

> [Twisting away, SHE smooths
> her clothes.
>   Enter BANNER.]

BANNER

Knox!

STURTEVANT

Help me, please help me!

BANNER

Swine!

> [Hits, kicks KNOX.]

KNOX

Don't, Banner! Don't!

BANNER

You monster. Monster. Monster. Monster. Flora, my darling, it's all right. You're safe now.

STURTEVANT

Frederick.

BANNER

Come with me.

[BANNER and STURTEVANT walk out, embracing.]

[BLACKOUT]

[END OF ACT THREE]

ACT FOUR

AT RISE, dusk, four days later.

HIS laboratory dismantled, KNOX is packing. Freezes at taps at door. Enter TOMMY.

KNOX

Tommy.

TOMMY

Cor! Going away?

KNOX

Yes, going away.

TOMMY

I'm sorry for it. Why?

KNOX

I am an evil man, Tommy.

TOMMY

Go on! Your serum what left me pure as a virgin? You're not so bad as most. Only one ever started with me who said get out.

KNOX

I bent Nature to my lust—with the usual tragic result.

TOMMY

Who with?

KNOX
Mr. Banner courageously allowed me to administer—

TOMMY
Mr. Banner, was it?

KNOX
I shouldn't have said. What are you here for? Money?

TOMMY
I want to go back posing for Mr. Banner, if you can help me with him.

KNOX
Surely other painters will hire you?

TOMMY
None have yet. It's a thin living in the best of times. See how skinny I'm getting? If not him, maybe you know a gentleman who likes his fun now and again?

[Brushes against KNOX.]

KNOX
That won't work with me, Tommy.

TOMMY
Paid already, if that makes you feel better.

KNOX
I mean I cannot.

TOMMY
Here, that serum didn't—?

KNOX
It poisoned me, Tommy. Damaged me irreparably.

TOMMY
Knew it was a barmy notion.

KNOX
Besides, your blood provided its basis, and that makes carnal relations with you impossible.

TOMMY [touching KNOX]
Bet this makes you hot.

KNOX
You don't know what I did. I forced the virtue of Miss Sturtevant.

TOMMY
When you couldn't with me?

KNOX
No more did I succeed with her, thank God!

TOMMY
What did you expect? It's the way we're made, you and me.

KNOX
Every touchstone of myself, every claim to moral standing, intellectual worth—lost!

TOMMY
You had no right. You should stick to your own kind.

KNOX
We're animals, beneath a veneer.

TOMMY

Right under our clothes.

[Works KNOX's groin. KNOX looks startled.]

There you go, Doctor! Tommy works the cure!

[Knocks heard.]

STURTEVANT [off]

Henry! Henry, let me in, I need to see you.

KNOX [to TOMMY]

Hide!

[TOMMY closes bed curtains as KNOX lets in STURTEVANT.]

Flora, I tried to see you — to apologize — but Miss Tiffin barred me. I am so sorry for what I did — so abjectly sorry.

[Kneels.]

I beg your forgiveness.

STURTEVANT

Oh Henry. I'm not angry. In a funny way — I'm not laughing at you — I'm glad it happened. No harm was done — be glad of that. If you were brutal, so is marriage brutal, and now we are saved from that. You are right to ask forgiveness, and I do forgive you. Henry, I must tell you how things have changed between Frederick — between Mr. Banner and myself.

KNOX

Banner!

STURTEVANT

I'm not fickle. You have been running away from me for years. I see that now, and I know my heart is one that must lodge close beside another's.

KNOX

I can never forgive myself.

STURTEVANT

I love him, Henry.

KNOX

Flora, I must tell you something terrible, something it would be wrong for me to hold back: Banner can never be a husband to you.

STURTEVANT

Unlike you, he wants to be.

KNOX

Oh God, it is my fault! I poisoned him, Flora. I made him into a—

[Off, BANNER calls "Flora! Flora!" Rushes on.]

BANNER

So help me, touch one hair of her head—

STURTEVANT

He did not molest me, Frederick.

KNOX
I understand I am to congratulate you.

BANNER
Flora! You accept?

[SHE nods.]

You make me the happiest man in the world.

TIFFIN [entering]
My dear, are you safe? I looked up and you were gone —

STURTEVANT
Quite safe.

BANNER
Miss Tiffin, congratulate us. I am unworthy of Flora, but we love each other.

STURTEVANT
With all our hearts.

TIFFIN
My dear! The son of an earl!

KNOX
Miss Tiffin, Flora has accepted my felicitations and my apology. I don't know what you know —

TIFFIN
Every particular.

BANNER
No need to rehearse the sordid details.

TIFFIN
That's all right, Mr. Banner. I know how in a drunken fit he offered to kiss Flora, and how you saved her. Your conduct stands out in bold relief from his. The age of chivalry is not dead!

GREENE [entering]
Doctor, the wagon will be here tomorrow morning at seven sharp.

BANNER
Mrs. Greene, congratulate us!

GREENE
You two? I thought it was the doctor. I *am* getting old. Now this is good news. I know you'll be happy.

STURTEVANT
Thank you, Mrs. Greene.

KNOX
Mrs. Greene, might I leave my chemical apparatus behind?

GREENE
In view of my trouble, I shall be forced to sell it.

KNOX
I quite understand. I need it no longer.

GREENE [to TIFFIN]
If you have any acquaintance in need of lodgings, Miss Toff— Toff— Mr. Banner can tell you how healthful this situation is, airy and convenient to Bedlam, perfect for gentleman *or* artist.

TIFFIN
I will keep it in mind, Mrs. Greene.

[To OTHERS:]

Call me old-fashioned, but I am disturbed when things break up for no sufficient apparent reason. A man does not resign his position without notice, dissolve his engagement and leave his lodgings because he got drunk. There must be more, and it would be a kindness to tell me what it is.

STURTEVANT
I wish you wouldn't pry.

TIFFIN
Mr. Banner?

STURTEVANT
Emily, really—

TIFFIN
Dr. Knox? Mrs. Greene, do *you* know what really happened?

GREENE
Ask me, I think Mr. Banner beat Dr. Knox. Close as brothers, but I'll wager if Dr. Knox did the wrong thing to an English gentleman of spirit, he'd have to pay the price.

TIFFIN
But what wrong thing did he *do?*

GREENE
No idea as to that. Unless— I have heard, but it's a horrible lie—

TIFFIN
What have you heard?

GREENE
Some do say that Dr. Knox gets 'em in here, dissects 'em, and *eats* 'em.

KNOX
Mrs. Greene!

BANNER [laughing]
Quite true.

TIFFIN
I assure you he does no such thing.

GREENE
Not saying he does.

TIFFIN
Mrs. Greene, with Dr. Knox's permission we will have our tea in here.

KNOX
Quite all right.

GREENE
Right away, miss, but it don't depend on his permission.

[Exits.]

TIFFIN
Dr. Knox, what wrong thing did you do to Mr. Banner?

KNOX
Miss Tiffin, it was an action, offered not to Mr. Banner, but to—

BANNER
I say, Knox, watch what you say.

STURTEVANT
Go ahead, Henry.

KNOX
I respect Miss Tiffin too much, Banner, to wish her left in the dark.

TIFFIN
Thank you, Dr. Knox.

KNOX
I attempted Miss Sturtevant's virtue.

BANNER
I knew Knox was depraved the first time I saw him eat fish. That his transgressions would not stop at using the wrong fork was to be predicted. It takes such a one to inflict shame on a lady—

KNOX
No shame adheres to Miss Sturtevant. Shame is mine alone. Only by confessing my action and repenting of it do I regain any tincture of self respect.

BANNER
You repent because you couldn't manage it?

STURTEVANT
Henry, you were going to tell me something about Frederick?

BANNER
What is it, Knox? Out with it! Nothing? I thought so!

TOMMY [emerging from bed]
He was going to say, Mr. Banner there, *he's* the sodomite!

TIFFIN
What!

BANNER
Tommy! You here?

TOMMY
Not fit to be her husband or any woman's.

KNOX
Tommy!

STURTEVANT
Oh!

BANNER
Wonderful, the very dirt speaks against me! This is flattering, Tommy. I hope I am not a snob, yet I take it as the highest compliment of which you are capable that you would slander me. Your avocation is blackmail? Against you I choose my one sufficient weapon: My word as a gentleman.

KNOX
Flora, Tommy does not know all. I must explain—

BANNER
As to the practices Tommy engages in, we might refer to Dr. Knox, in whose rooms he evidently feels at home.

KNOX
Oh God, Flora, this is what I wanted to explain.

TOMMY
He means his bloody serum.

STURTEVANT
What serum is that?

KNOX
An experiment gone terribly wrong. Banner cannot be a husband to you, Flora, or to any woman, for I have poisoned him.

TIFFIN
In layman's language, please.

KNOX
My research has focused on sodomy — the condition wherein a man loves other men.

BANNER
Knox can tell you how he overcame my resistance.

KNOX
I corrupted him. I devised a serum — this serum. It impels any man who drinks of it to perform acts of animal congress with members of his own sex! I drank it, and Banner did me — did mankind — the service of drinking it also.

TIFFIN
Why would you want to wreak such evil upon the human race?

STURTEVANT
Frederick, why would you swallow such a potion?

TOMMY
Potion!

KNOX
My aim was to cure the affliction—

BANNER
Knox, you forget that I took the antidote, too.

TIFFIN
Antidote?

BANNER
The cure. You see, Flora, there was no reason to speak of a temporary misadventure.

KNOX
The antidote failed. I took it to no effect. My theory that the serum promised its own reversal proved false.

BANNER
You gave me the antidote, Knox, and by God it did work. Flora, I can prove it!

KNOX
I never gave it to you, Banner. God forgive me, when you drank what I said was the cure, I was giving you more serum.

BANNER
Then by God give me the antidote now.

STURTEVANT
You say you have no need —

BANNER
No, no, no. No more do I. The fact is, his serum had no effect but to turn my stomach — a vile-tasting liqueur that made me shudder and vomit. It's an aperient, nothing more. An utter failure so far as his lascivious purpose was concerned. His poison failed and so requires no antidote. You believe me, don't you?

TIFFIN
We much prefer to.

BANNER
It needed but this: I stand accused by a man whose fiancée prefers me. It's a story out of Frankenstein: Losing control over losing control.

STURTEVANT
This explains — Emily, you remember when we found them in bed? Henry's one, too!

TIFFIN
Dr. Knox, you admit that you ingested this — this love potion?

KNOX
I do.

TIFFIN
And did it — move your concupiscence? Did you and Mr. Banner — ?

KNOX

We did.

BANNER

A lie!

TIFFIN

Child, I feel sick. Tell us, Dr. Knox, have you had — relations — with any other — ?

KNOX

I would rather not say.

TOMMY

Dr. Knox is a friend of mine, miss.

BANNER

Tommy, what we want to know is: Did Dr. Knox ever fiddle with your privates?

STURTEVANT

Frederick!

KNOX

Have some consideration, Banner.

TOMMY

The doctor did nothing with me he need regret.

BANNER

Is the doctor a sod? Tell us: Yes or no?

[To TIFFIN:]

The truth will reconcile Mr. Sturtevant to the loss of his prospective son-in-law.

TOMMY

If I am what you say, I find nothing to complain of.

BANNER

I asked about Knox.

[TOMMY is silent.]

Get out, you baggage.

TOMMY

Turn my stomach, you hypocrite. The answer, the true answer, is Mr. Banner's the sod! And was that before ever he met Dr. Knox!

BANNER

Out! You blinking little bugger!

TIFFIN

Stop! What is he saying?

TOMMY

If it's the way I'm made, it's the way he is too. Many a night we lay together, till the doctor came along.

KNOX

Is this true?

BANNER

It's a damned filthy lie!

[To TOMMY:]

Damn you, you dirty —

KNOX

What a backward glare of falsity. I feel sick.

TOMMY

Wasn't nothing wrong with it.

KNOX

No, no, I don't blame you.

BANNER

I've had mistresses as well. One does, you know. Flora needn't worry that she's getting a husband different from other husbands.

KNOX [to BANNER]

But I was in love with you.

[Sensation.]

TOMMY

Worse luck for you.

BANNER

This is worse than absurd, it is offensive. The time has come to fetch the constable to apprehend Knox on a charge of attempted rape!

STURTEVANT

Henry, you say — in love?

KNOX

When one heart opens to another, is that not beautiful?

TIFFIN

That depends.

KNOX [to BANNER]

When you were near, I was aware only of you, and when you weren't, all I thought about was you. At night I pressed against the length of you, my skin slipping along yours with edgings of fire.

BANNER

Damn you.

KNOX

Are you so lost to yourself? What was I thinking? I can put my hand through you. Oh God, Flora, you do lose out.

[STURTEVANT goes to BANNER.
Enter GREENE.]

GREENE

Here we go, nice hot tea!

STURTEVANT

He can change with a woman's love. That I know. Frederick, I come to you with all my loyalty, all my love.

BANNER

Dearest!

KNOX [laughing]

Oh Lord, I am slow! Banner, your history means my serum is useless — absolutely useless, no more magical than Mrs. Greene's tea, if — I grant you — stronger tasting.

GREENE
Here! I will not stand by —

BANNER
But look at its effect on you.

KNOX
You explained that: My serum was the long way round to what I really wanted.

BANNER
Knox, you disgust us. High time you got out. You are insane.

KNOX
Nature gives us one good: Vitality. She leaves it to us to learn that what promotes vitality is good, what saps it bad. It's no gift of my serum that makes me want a man. I come by that naturally.

TOMMY
Now you're talking.

STURTEVANT
All your work has gone for naught?

KNOX
Wasted? No: Not wasted, for my serum did help bridge my wishes and my behavior, helped to animate my body with my own spirit. I have learned to trust my heart. Mine is not after all the Greek sin of hubris —

BANNER
Rather, the Hebraic one of sodomy.

TIFFIN
The detestable and abominable sin amongst Christians not to be named.

KNOX
Tommy?

TOMMY
Sir?

KNOX
My name is Henry.

TOMMY
Yes, 'Enery?

KNOX
I want you.

GREENE [dropping tray]
Is he drunk again?

TOMMY
Yes, 'Enery, that'll do for a start. Where're we off to, then?

KNOX
Home to America. That sound all right to you?

TOMMY
You'll be a mad-doctor there?

KNOX
Yes.

TOMMY
Are there many lunatics?

KNOX
Practically the entire population.

TOMMY
They need keepers as well as doctors?

KNOX
They do.

TOMMY
Sounds good to me, then.

BANNER
He'll be your keeper, Knox?

TOMMY
My brother's—

KNOX
Frederick, the love of a man for a man does not reside in the blood. I was wrong about that. It comes from the root, the marrow, the soul you claim I have no belief in. Your disavowal of desire is as grievous as your disavowal of the ideal.

BANNER
Your perverted ideal? Greek love is unnatural—except for Greeks.

KNOX
If more innocent times once were, they existed innocently.

STURTEVANT
The ideal has no place in life.

TIFFIN
Child!

BANNER
Knox, your Tommy hasn't any human qualities. He's an animal. If you don't freeze him by staring into those empty eyes, he will cut your throat in the night.

KNOX
I like him.

BANNER
Poor Knox. It is its own worst punishment.

STURTEVANT
Henry, can't you discover a true cure?

KNOX
Flora, love is no disease. Rather, love cures our fatal loneliness. My need was for a man, and I may have found him.

BANNER
You want the woman in Tommy — his mobile hips, his smile and eyes at odds with each other.

KNOX
I like him for the man he is, hips, lips, eyes and everything.

STURTEVANT
What do sodomites *do?*

TOMMY
Don't you fret about that.

KNOX
I have faith in the body.

BANNER
Knox, you are a monstrous, misshapen thing.

STURTEVANT
Write to Uncle Cleve, won't you?

[Turns away, attended by BANNER.]

KNOX [to TOMMY]
The Elgin marbles are not more beautiful than you.

TOMMY
Cold, aren't they? Nice to look at, but to do the deed, give me flesh and blood.

TIFFIN
Have we been transported to Bedlam, to be subjected to such crazy talk? Mrs. Greene, you will send for the constable at once.

GREENE
I will that, and gladly. Count the silver! To think such filth in my house! You do yourself proud, miss. Afraid of your other engagement from the beginning. Dr. Knox is pleasing to look at but strange—always shut up, thinking, studying, tapping his pencils. Not natural. Says to meself, *Beware, Mr. Mad-Doctor, beware catching madness at Bedlam!*

[Exits.]

TOMMY
'Enery! Time we got going!

KNOX
I am a man. I can take it.

TOMMY
Don't be a fool! Let's you and me be leaving!

[Grabs KNOX, heads for door, throws *In Memoriam* at pursuing BANNER.]

TIFFIN
Not leave: You are cast out. Consider and repent!

[Door slams.]

BANNER [opening door]
Run! We're after you, Knox! And we'll get you! Society hovers over you like a bird of prey, ready to pounce and kill! Run!

[Closes door, turns.]

Sods should be dealt with as in olden days: Drawn and quartered, privates cut off and stuffed in their mouths, then hanged, cut down, revived and cut into pieces. That is what their love-making should bring down on them. There, there, Flora, no need to think of him again. He'll live a cold and lonely life, outcast and despised — he and his keeper.

TIFFIN

Make her happy, Mr. Banner. Your bride is the loveliest girl in the world. The grace of her form, the charm of her mind — too purely feminine, I have often thought, for the marriage bed. I will miss you, dear. I have come to love you more than any sister. Pay no mind to me, I'm being silly. Come away upstairs.

[Exits.
BANNER opens windows
to darkness.]

BANNER

Get some air in here. Ah, dark already! How things change.

[STURTEVANT, holding HER stomach, goes to windows, breathes, as BANNER opens *In Memoriam*.]

In the mood for Tennyson, my dear?

[Reads from Section 56:]

Man, her last work, who seem'd so fair,
  Such splendid purpose in his eyes,
Who roll'd the psalm to wintry skies,
  Who built him fanes of fruitless prayer,

Who trusted God was love indeed
  And love Creation's final law —
Tho' Nature, red in tooth and claw
  With raven, shriek'd against his creed —

. . . O life as futile, then, as frail!
  O for thy voice to soothe and bless!

What hope of answer, or redress?
  Behind the veil, behind the veil.

                    [Moves to embrace
                    STURTEVANT.]

                    STURTEVANT
Don't touch me.

                    [BLACKOUT]

                    [END OF PLAY]

AND OTHER PLAYS AND ADAPTATIONS –

One-Act Plays

– *A JOURNAL OF THE PLAGUE YEAR,*

AND OTHER PLAYS AND ADAPTATIONS –

The Happy Ending

A Play in Two Scenes

The Happy Ending

CAST OF CHARACTERS

LEAFLETTER: Young man.

OLD AGITATOR: Older man in work clothes.

PEDESTRIANS

SCENE AND TIME

Scene One

Sunny afternoon sidewalk on Manhattan's West 23rd Street.

Scene Two

Same, an hour later.

SCENE ONE

AT RISE, LEAFLETTER stands listlessly, a leaflet fluttering from HIS hand, others held at HIS side.

PEDESTRIANS pass, ignoring HIM. OLD AGITATOR walks past. Stops to watch, then comes up.

OLD AGITATOR

Hey, guy, that's not how you do it! That's not the way! Hardly noticed you! Walked right past! Want everyone to walk past? People'll help you out, but first they got to see you. Don't hold it limp, waiting for them to come to you—wave it in their face, put it in their hands. Got to break through! Hey, give me, I'll show you. Don't worry: You look like a nice guy.

> [Takes leaflets, waves one at passing PEDESTRIAN, who accepts it.]

Got to sell it, see: *Sell*. You know "sell"? Make 'em notice you, make 'em want it in their hot little hands—want it in the worst way. Give it some *oomph,* let 'em know you mean business.

> [Lodges another leaflet with passing PEDESTRIAN. Light on HIS feet, turning to catch every passerby, OLD AGITATOR rapidly hands out leaflets. Most drop them; none reads them.

Pedestrian stream dries up.]

See you guys on the street, dozens every day, and it's like you're fresh off the boat, just off the bus, someone says, *"Here,"* and there you stand, not an idea in your head how to do it. You got to *sell*. That's the whole secret of the American Dream. Put it into their hands, their heads. Know where they *really* got to want it. . . ? *Hmmmm?* You can imagine, I won't say.

But that's the job. Hang back in the woodwork, you're not doing it right. This is New York, plenty to ignore already. Everyone's busy blocking out. And if they ignore you, how you going to eat? Long as you got to hand out fliers, by God, be the best damn flier-hander-outer in the business. That's *my* philosophy.

[PEDESTRIAN accepts leaflet.]

Learned how years ago. Every strike in town — and it was a union town then — every strike I was out here on the street with the local, handing out leaflets, letting the people know about the bosses, how they'd starve you soon as look at you, work you six days a week, *seven* if they could get away with it, no overtime, starvation wages, and bilk you out of 'em if they could, scare you so bad you never give a peep of complaint, or if you do, you're on the blacklist.

Yeah, got in trouble now and then, but people pulled together in those days, changes got made. Reforms. Yeah, solidarity! Fight the bosses, fight the scabs, help the *work*-ing man. Yeah, take it,

[PEDESTRIAN accepts leaflet.]

help the cause, fight the bosses, fight the scabs, help the *work*-ing man, help the *work*-ing woman.

> [PEDESTRIANS accept leaflets.]

Check it out: Strike!

> [PEDESTRIANS take leaflets at every iteration of "Strike!"]

Strike! Strike! Strike! Strike! Strike!

> [Pedestrian stream dries up.]

Think you got it? Take over, give it a try.

> [Hands over leaflets, watches LEAFLETTER stand inert as before, PEDESTRIANS ignoring HIM.]

No, no, no, no, *no*. Sell it. *Sell* it. Let me. Watch close.

> [Takes leaflets.]

OK, see this guy stepping away?

> [Approaching PEDESTRIAN swerves.]

I take a step, intercept: *bam!*

> [PEDESTRIAN accepts leaflet.]

That's *sellin'*, see? Figure out their pattern, put yourself smack in the way. That's the whole secret. Stick together, we'll be all right. OK, here comes a lady. Watch.

> [Holds out leaflet as FEMALE
> PEDESTRIAN approaches,
> swerves.]

Bam!

> [SHE refuses leaflet.]

Damn. Well, there's always one.

> [PEDESTRIANS pass, ignoring
> OLD AGITATOR.]

OK, so one or two turn up their nose. Don't bother me, fought against their kind my whole life, got up at meetings, let the people know they're out here, walking over us like we're bugs on the sidewalk, *clip*-ping their *cou*-pons and *cash*-ing their *checks* earned by the sweat of the *work*-ing man's brow.

Oh man, put a jinx on me? C'mon, people, got something for you. Don't be afraid, I don't bite. Think I'm a goddam scab? Never! No way! I'm one of you. C'mon! Taking food out of the mouths of babies here.

> [Stands forlorn, ignored, until a
> PEDESTRIAN plucks leaflet
> from HIS inert hand.]

Thanks, brother: *Thank* you! Always darkest before dawn. Keep the faith! C'mon, help the struggle, help the cause, fight the bosses, fight the scabs, help the *work*-ing man, help the *work*-ing woman, help your *bro*-ther and your *sis*-ter, your *bro*-ther and your *sis*-ter. *Strike!*

> [Adding grinding hip motion to HIS approach, PEDESTRIANS accept leaflets at every iteration of "Strike!"]

Strike! Strike! Strike! Strike! Strike! That's it, people! That's the spirit, we'll show 'em yet! See, guy, it's cause I'm sellin' it — *sellin'* it!

I'm hot! When you're hot you're hot! It's that ol' sex appeal. Sex appeal makes the world go round. It's all sex! Hey hey hey! Let's boogie! Get down! Oh yeah! Sex!

> [PEDESTRIANS take leaflets at every iteration of "Sex!"]

Sex! Sex! Sex! Sex! Sex!

> [Pedestrian stream dries up.]

Hoo boy! Takes it out of you. Take over now? Think you got it? Got what it takes? Show me what you got.

> [Hands over leaflets to LEAFLETTER, watches HIM stand inert.]

C'mon, move your hips — it's all in the hips.

> [Demonstrates.]

Got to *sell* it.

> [Shakes head, smiles.]

Ah, just don't get it, do you? Well, keep trying, who knows, maybe it'll come to you. Doubt it, but you never know. What're we selling here, anyway? Pressman's strike? The hotel workers? Nail salon? Cut-rate suits?

> [Puts on reading glasses, peers at leaflet.]

Huh! "Girlfriends of the Orient. Discreet massage for tired executive. Well-educated ladies know secrets of the East with aromatic herbs." Oh Jesus...

> [Stuffs leaflet in shirt.]

Say, where *is* this place?

> [LEAFLETTER points upwards.]

Upstairs, eh? Yeah, well, good luck to you. Nice working with you. Welcome to America! Fight the goddam bosses!

> [Raises fist and exits, looking upwards with anticipation.
> LEAFLETTER stands with leaflet fluttering from HIS hand as PEDESTRIANS pass, ignoring HIM.]
>
> [BLACKOUT]
>
> [END OF SCENE ONE]

SCENE TWO

(N.B. Best played after one or more intervening one-act plays.)

AT RISE, LEAFLETTER stands listlessly. OLD AGITATOR enters wearing apron like a newsvendor's, stamped "SEX SEX SEX SEX," sniffing HIS fingers, slicking back hair.

     OLD AGITATOR [reaching for leaflets]
OK, buddy, I'll take over now.

    [No response. Grabs leaflets.]

You can go. Hear me? Take a load off! Go home! Get it? You're through! Sorry to be the one to tell you, but it's a dog eat dog world, and I got to eat, too. What can I do, they know class when they see it? Educated ladies! Like I told you — I was honest — you got to be the best. They made an offer, I made an offer, we reached an agreement, shook on it.

Hey, wake up and smell the coffee! Time to go! Beat it!

    [Begins handing leaflets to
    passing MALE PEDESTRIANS,
    leering at FEMALE
    PEDESTRIANS).]

Dream job. Fringe benefits I been fighting for since I was a kid. Talk about a happy ending! Oh do those girls know their stuff.

Hoo-boy. Feel young again. Feel great! Unless—unless I got the Jersey kiss?

> [Looks sick, feels crotch, considers, cheers up.]

Nah, they looked clean. OK, buddy, get lost. Let the master do it. *Yo!* Check it out!

> [MALE PEDESTRIANS accept leaflets.]

Check it out, got it for you right here. Know what you want, guy, and it's right up the stairs— Yessir, golden fingers of the East, what it's *all* about, *hoo-ee*. Yo! Check it out, buddy. Want a girl? Want a date?

> [To LEAFLETTER:]

Get lost, kid, you're history. Can't you see I'm busy?

> [To MALE PEDESTRIAN:]

Want a girl? Want a date? Massage?

> [To LEAFLETTER:]

Hey, tried to help, you weren't interested. Survival of the fittest, buddy: Ever hear of it? Clear the sidewalk there, let 'em by. You learned something, be happy! Step along.

> [Exit LEAFLETTER as PEDESTRIANS pass.]

Help the cause, fight the bosses, fight the scabs, help the *work*-ing man, help the *work*-ing woman. *Strike! Strike! Strike!*

[To PEDESTRIAN:]

Hey, buddy — want it? Course you do! You know what I'm talking about. Second floor front.

[PEDESTRIAN accepts leaflet.]

Help the *work*-ing man, help the *work*-ing girl, help the *work*-ing girl! Want a date? Check it out, check it out! *Strike! Strike! Strike! Strike! Strike!*

[BLACKOUT]

[END OF PLAY]

– A JOURNAL OF THE PLAGUE YEAR,

AND OTHER PLAYS AND ADAPTATIONS –

My Gamaliel

A Play in Two Scenes

My Gamaliel

CAST OF CHARACTERS

MATTIE: Fisherman's wife, drawn-looking though not yet 30.

NELMA: Mattie's boarder, a pretty 19-year-old.

SCENE AND TIME

Scene One

Kitchen of MATTIE's house near Seward's harbor, the morning of July 15, 1923. Rocking chair and stool flank stove. Window, rear, to green and purple hills; door and window, right. Doorway, left.

Scene Two

Same, half an hour later.

SCENE ONE

AT RISE, blasts from locomotive whistle. MATTIE knits, rocking. On stool, NELMA listens wide-eyed.

MATTIE
There. That will be his train. Can you find me the green yarn, Nelma?

NELMA
Wish I could be at the station. I've never seen a President of the United States. Don't they at least have a band?

MATTIE
No band. As the Mayor said, any town can give him a band. Seward's giving him a special honor: going about our business as usual. The Mayor will shake President Harding's hand, then slip discreetly away.

NELMA
I don't see why we have to stay inside.

[Hands yarn, goes to window.]

MATTIE
Respect. Lets him see the place without a fuss. And it tells him we in Alaska think pretty well of ourselves.

NELMA
I'd throw him a picnic. I would, on the Custom House lawn. Shoot off the cannon. Fireworks. Parade. Put on some pomp.

MATTIE
That's you all over, Nelma. But he gets treated that way every place. The Mayor's idea displays true hospitality. Shows the President we consider him family.

NELMA
And he's the black sheep?

MATTIE [joining NELMA]
Self reliance is thrust on every one of us up here.

NELMA
They'll be sorry they missed this, Tom and Bill.

MATTIE
Won't give it a second thought while the salmon are running.

NELMA
When will they be back?

MATTIE
Child, you ask me that every day. I don't know. When the boat's full of fish.

NELMA
I come up here a bride and in a month I might as well be a widow.

MATTIE
It's hard, being a fisherman's wife. I'm glad you're in my house.

NELMA
That's sweet of you, Mattie. Look! I see him!

[Points.]

Look over there!

MATTIE
President Warren G. Harding! What a distinguished figure! Like a bull! Such an august profile!

NELMA
Mattie, he's handsome!

[Pause.]

He's gone. There was no one around him. He was by himself.

[MATTIE sits down, resumes knitting. NELMA stays at window.]

MATTIE
Today is Seward's red letter day. I am so proud. But worn out. The kids already wore me out today, Little Bill running all over the place, excited, and the girls catching it and screaming bloody murder. Thank goodness Mrs. Tucker said send them over.

NELMA
One month, and I've seen my first bear, conceived my first child, and now had my first sight of a President.

MATTIE
Wish you'd see the doctor. Make sure.

NELMA

The only thing he can tell me is when, and I don't care when. I've had this feeling almost since the wedding. It's wonderful. Magic.

MATTIE

Nelma?

> [Indicates yarn. Sitting where SHE can look out window, NELMA puts out HER hands, MATTIE places skein of yarn over them, begins winding it into a ball.]

A child would settle you. Your Tom, his first wife always wanted babies, God rest her soul. Never had any.

NELMA

Oh, my first bear was such a sight. Day before the boys left, Tom took me up in the hills. Felt heavy as lead, the slopes were so steep. We finally reached a cleft where minute pools were swarming with life. I could look up at snowcapped peaks and a turquoise glacier, then down into jungles crawling with bugs and tiny fish. Of course being from California I had to have snow, so we went on up to it. It was so strange. Know what Tom called it?

MATTIE

What?

NELMA

Rotten snow. More the memory of snow than snow. Honeycombed with air. A frozen spider's web, but as you watch, the edges aren't there any more. Coming down we saw what I took for a mangy old sheep dog, only six times as big, with a big swollen head. So naked. I wasn't a bit scared, but Tom says I should have been.

                        MATTIE

It ran, though, didn't it?

                        NELMA

Yes.

                        MATTIE

Bears generally do.

                        NELMA

And way below we could see Seward, neatly laid out like a little toy town.

                        MATTIE

That's what it was ten years ago when I was a greenhorn. Few shacks and not more than a hundred people.

                        NELMA

It's grown?

                        MATTIE

Out of recognition. *My* first grizzly I saw on Main Street. Rude shock for a well brought-up young lady. It's entirely sprung up since then—streets and houses, stores and docks.

                        NELMA

Mattie, I've never seen a smaller place. When the boat docked and Tom said we were there and we were *here*, I wanted to cry.

MATTIE

Pshaw, girl. Have to be made of stern stuff if you expect to last in Alaska. Show some gumption. Small town but a big place. Mark my words: When they start hauling out the ore, the timber, the pelts, when they get their canneries built, and the warehouses, why, that bay's going to resemble a Chicago freight yard. The racket will be incessant, and what with locomotives and steamers and automobiles, smoke will plume up over Seward like the feather in our cap.

NELMA

Wish I could be so optimistic. So small.

MATTIE

Hasn't been a bear seen in town this year *or* last. And I and the other members of the Ladies Club do what we can to improve things. Why, the new picket fence around the Custom House is our doing. Painted it snow white the last of May.

NELMA

Couldn't the Ladies Club give a reception for the President?

MATTIE

Wouldn't be proper.

NELMA

Proper!

MATTIE

The Mayor decreed, and the council backed him up, that we would honor the President by not bothering him. The Ladies Club won't defy that edict. Our purpose is to promote such precepts, not defy them.

NELMA
Well, one day a bronze statue of Warren G. Harding twice life size will stand looking up at the mountains where he found the Promised Land. And today is the day it will commemorate. At the unveiling we'll have a band, and a picnic, and speeches, crowds of people, fireworks and whistles and cannon.

MATTIE [smiling]
I'm sure you will. And the Ladies Club will fence it in.

[MATTIE finishing ball of yarn, NELMA pops up to window, points.]

NELMA
Mattie, there he is again, at the corner. Sitting down on the curb to rest. Don't you just want to ask him in, offer him some tea?

MATTIE
No.

NELMA
Warren G. Harding. Wonder what the G is for. Look at him. Weight of the world on his shoulders. Poor lamb. No idea which way to turn.

[Backs away from window, blushing.]

Oh! He couldn't be staring at me!

[*sotto voce*]

No! Don't go away!

[MATTIE pulls NELMA away
from window, pulls curtains.]

MATTIE

Enough. Don't bother him.

NELMA

I didn't do anything.

MATTIE

You're so pretty, you don't need to do anything.

NELMA

He seems alone in a far wilderness.

[MATTIE peeks through
curtains, takes out a skein of
lilac yarn and sits down.]

MATTIE

He'll get by. Conserving his energy. Learn that fast up here. Fool Nature into thinking you have no reserve, then live off that reserve all winter. Plenty for him to see. We're a small but scenic town. He'll be occupied for some little time if he intends to admire the whole of Seward.

NELMA

Sometimes your eyes get so bright, Mattie. The thought of winter chills me.

[Pause.]

It's cruel, ignoring him.

MATTIE

Nelma?

[NELMA sitting down reluctantly, MATTIE places skein of yarn over HER hands, winds it into a ball.]

He's only a man. Alaska treats everybody the same. Why else the snow and ice and unbalanced days and nights, the distance, mountains, bears and mosquitoes? It's here for you, but you have to find it and hold on until you break through. Alaska won't make it easy for any man or woman.

NELMA [yawning]

I am so all in. Don't know how you can sleep in broad daylight. Last night I couldn't close my eyes until two a.m., when the light finally faded, but the sun woke me up again at 4:30.

MATTIE

My Lord, Nelma, no one sleeps in the summertime. No one wants to miss a minute! The juices flow so long as there's light in the sky. It does get to you. By August people are so cranky. When he's home Bill stays up all night so he can read the paper on the front porch by sunlight at three a.m. That's his principal delight, reading the paper on the front porch at three a.m. by sunlight.

NELMA

I thought, ice and snow, polar bears, a bitter wind, long dark nights. Then I get here and it's light around the clock, grass up to my waist and birds chirping monkey sounds. No North Pole about it.

MATTIE
Our garden produce beats anything in the Lower Forty-Eight. You'll have your fill of the dark this winter.

NELMA
What's winter like, Mattie?

MATTIE
Long, dark and cold. Bay freezes over. Nothing moves but the steady drift of snow and ice. Winter's when you stay indoors and raise your family.

NELMA
I hope Tom doesn't get tired of me.

MATTIE
Winter is the Alaskan season. You close up, seal life inside of you and get your rest. I love it.

NELMA
Do you?

MATTIE
In the summer I tire myself out trying to civilize this patch of ground. Simpler in winter. Get the family fed, pack the kids off to school, and rest. Everything outside kind of dissolves. Go deep inside myself. I have a good man, too, I'll say that. Nothing beats winter for finding out. Then when you cannot take any more of it, it flips again. Summer comes round, just as extreme, sun hammering, and life bursts out. You repair your fences and build more. Every year we put out new outposts of propriety, new flowerbeds, fences and sidewalks. It shows we have survived.

NELMA
I hate it here. There's nothing here for me. I want to leave. I'll burst if I stay.

MATTIE
Patience, child. You're young, you want to nail down your future once and for all. But you can't. Can't be done. What you need is patience, give up some of your ideas, learn how to reconcile the short summer with eternal winter.

NELMA
You're old and settled. You can do without. You're worn out. I'm too young to settle for living at the edge of things.

MATTIE
Not worn out: Made strong. I've seen blizzards and tidal waves. Once in an earthquake I saw the ground open up and knew the end of the world had come. That's a volcano out there, and I'm ready for when it wakes up.

NELMA
You're just weathered. Life's scoured you down to an essence, Mattie, worn you to a nub. Life's doing the carving. You're just doing the enduring.

MATTIE
I am living my life as I see fit. Alaska's been good to me, but life's not easy here or any place else.

NELMA
Well, Alaska is not for me.

MATTIE
Nelma!

[NELMA throws down yarn,
strides towards door. MATTIE
restrains HER.]

NELMA [collapsing in MATTIE's
arms]

Oh Mattie, I'm sorry! Don't know what comes over me. It's only, there's nothing here to take me out of myself.

MATTIE

It's all right, Nelma, it's all right. You only just arrived. Can't be expected yet to know how we cope, throw ourselves outwards in the summer, draw ourselves in for the winter.

NELMA

With my baby.

MATTIE

Well, we'll see. . . Winter does that.

NELMA [opening curtains]

There's the President! Oh Mattie, what's happened to him? He looks wounded. Like a little boy the bigger ones tell to go home. I wish you'd ask him in, Mattie. Show him the clean and decent house you keep. I baked sourdough bread last night. It's still warm.

MATTIE

Upset his stomach. He's running.

[Looks out, opens window,
leans out.]

Hey! Hey you boys! Leave him alone!

NELMA [calling]
Get away from him or I'll scratch your eyes out, filthy ragamuffins!

[To MATTIE:]

How dare they throw rocks! Cruel, cruel boys! Nasty! Someone should wring their necks.

MATTIE
He has seen worse, I dare say. Boys will be boys.

NELMA
But that's not right.

MATTIE [sitting down]
Alaskans are individualists. If the President learns only that, he's ahead of the game. All he ever gets in Washington is tea at Mrs. Longworth's, a ball at Mrs. McLean's. Seward must appear attractive to him. We painted the house special. Year early but I told my Bill, I'll die if the President sees our faded old paint, let's freshen up. Most everyone did.

NELMA
There's a something in his eyes. Slightly wild. Lonely.

[Gasps.]

MATTIE
What is it, Nelma?

NELMA
Miz Pritchard has her head out the window.

MATTIE

Hussy! I know what she's up to. Enticing the President!

[Thrusts head out window.]

Get back inside, Miranda, you know better than that. Remember what the Mayor said! You have no right!

[To NELMA:]

The nerve of that woman. Thought she might be up to something, she was baking yesterday and the day before, and I wondered who on earth does Miranda Pritchard expect to drop by?

NELMA

The nerve!

MATTIE [sitting down]

Never short of that. Takes advantage. We have a nice little community here, very democratic, but you always get someone with airs who thinks the rules don't apply, that *she* can give the President a cup of tea if she wants to, no matter what the Mayor decreed.

NELMA

Truly shocking.

MATTIE

Come to that, he'd prefer my raisin cookies to her tired old pound cake.

NELMA

So he would. My Tom says, "Why can't you make raisin cookies as good as Mattie's?"

MATTIE
Well, few can. Not to boast.

NELMA
Mattie, he's back! Knocking at Miz Pritchard's back door. She's letting him in!

[MATTIE flies to door, opens it.]

MATTIE
You, Miranda: I told you, you can't let him in there. The Mayor will hear of this!

[Goes off right. NELMA watches until MATTIE returns half a minute later, sits down.]

That was close.

NELMA [restlessly roaming]
The President didn't look so happy.

MATTIE
Told me he's hungry and thirsty. I said to rough it. Just watching out for *her*. She'd never live it down.

NELMA
What do you mean?

MATTIE
Why, she's a maiden lady, Nelma. She would have found life in Seward insupportable. She'll thank me. Eventually. They do say he likes the ladies.

NELMA

Still, for the distinction...

MATTIE

Notoriety, you mean.

NELMA

What woman wouldn't? More power to her, Mattie. She could emerge as Seward's leading hostess. Worth the try. I'd do the same.

MATTIE

Not in my house, you wouldn't. Won't bring shame down on me! Think it's pound cake the man's on the prowl for?

NELMA

Mattie, you're frostbitten! You're rotten snow! You and your endless seasonal round, throwing yourself out and drawing back in, like a crazy top someone's thrown on the floor.

[Tense pause.]

He's sitting down again. Looking at the houses.

[Shies back from window.]

Everyone's standing back in the shadows, pulling down the shades. Must think it's a ghost town.

MATTIE [joining NELMA]

Strange to be President. Woodrow Wilson's never been the same.

[Pause.]

He does look a little peaked.

      NELMA [sob in voice]
Looks so frustrated. So needy. Like he's going to cry.

      MATTIE
Gumption, Mr. President!

      NELMA
Oh, Mattie, can't we have him in for tea? A proper tea? Two married women together? He's glancing this way. He's getting up! He's coming over! Walking like a broken man.

      MATTIE [putting arm around
      NELMA]
Shambling just like a grizzly bear. Deceptive, probably.

      [Pause. At knocks on door,
      NELMA shies back.]

      NELMA [whimpering]
Mattie!

      [More knocks.]

      MATTIE [galvanized]
All right, child. Go on in there.

      [NELMA composes HERSELF,
      exits left. Through window:]

Not this door. Around back, if you please, Mr. President. Around back!

– A JOURNAL OF THE PLAGUE YEAR,

[Exit left. Sounds of door opening and closing. MATTIE returns, pulls curtains of both windows to, then, addressing neighbor, exits right.]

Miranda Pritchard, how dare you have the audacity to defy the clearly stated wish of the Mayor and town council and deliberately entice. . .

[BLACKOUT]

[END OF SCENE ONE]

SCENE TWO

AT RISE, MATTIE knits in rocking chair to the frantic and accelerating rhythm of bedsprings, off, which stops as teakettle whistles.
 Pours tea, arranges plate of cookies.

MATTIE
Oh my. Sun's breaking through, wreathed in smiles of peace. Innocent and fresh. Clouds have moved aside, and the slopes show the sun moving rapidly across, kicking up its coverlet near the end of a late sleep. The water's sparkling, a million chromium slivers. How pretty.

 [Door slams, off.]

Well, I *am* old—old enough to have my own tried ideas of what's worthwhile in this world. This is for the best. Nelma wants to stay, really, if only she can. This will permit her to do so. Something to turn to, a warmth inside her. Alaska calls upon interior resources. Yes, life's chipped freely away at me, she's right, but there's more, now, of me to carve away than there used to be.

 [NELMA enters languorously,
 exquisitely self-aware.]

NELMA
The *G* stands for Gamaliel! My Gamaliel!

MATTIE

Here's a cup of tea.

NELMA [at window]

Mattie, now I *know* I'm with child. Now I am certain. It's as if he left himself with me. As if he gave up his spirit. Mattie, thank you. I was so surprised.

MATTIE [going to window]

Did it without thinking. Couldn't fight it.

[Ship's whistle blasts, joined by others.]

NELMA

Never thought you'd let him in.

MATTIE

Had to, child. Formality, reserve—they let you know where you are. But when it comes to people pairing off—put etiquette aside and stand back. Propriety does not apply to anything so ridiculous. That is a silly thing of contrivance and compulsion and disclosure of the heart. You wanting to serve him tea! But it lets life go on, and you have a right to your happiness. Child, opening the door to your Gamaliel was the only *proper* thing I could do. Now, have your tea.

[Sits down, holds up knitting.]

Won't this be pretty? My favorite colors—suitable for either a baby boy or a baby girl.

NELMA

Oh Mattie.

[THEY embrace.]

[BLACKOUT]

[END OF PLAY]

– A JOURNAL OF THE PLAGUE YEAR,

AND OTHER PLAYS AND ADAPTATIONS –

The Garden Party

A Comedy in One Scene

– A JOURNAL OF THE PLAGUE YEAR,

The Garden Party

CAST OF CHARACTERS

CYNTHIA: An imposing beauty of 45 or 50, moving with pantherly confidence in a purple jumpsuit.

DEXTER: Cynthia's impeccably groomed young husband.

HARRY: Mid-60s, ravaged ruin in butler's uniform.

MAGGIE: Harry's pretty wife, 60, in cook's dress pinks.

BOBBY: Harry's 17-year-old underling, draped in an old uniform of Harry's.

SCENE AND TIME

A Westchester mansion's pantry on a Saturday afternoon in June. Doorway left, table center, swinging door right. Curtained storage pantry, rear.

AT RISE, counters are laden with cakes, pitchers of punch, piles of fruit. On floor, tub of iced Champagne bottles.

With BOBBY's help, HARRY arranges trays and carries them off right with pitchers of punch, punctuating every trip by recourse to a glass on a counter.

Off, the sound of the garden party rises through the usual stages, from polite reluctant murmurs to lively conversation, hilarity and, finally, raucous drunken abandon.

HARRY

All right, they got punch. They got petits fours.

[snaps fingers]

Where're the cucumber sandwiches? Bobby, tell Maggie to get 'em out there. Once the punch hits, they won't want cucumber any more.

BOBBY

Yessir.

[Exits left. HARRY slices fruit as CYNTHIA and DEXTER enter right.]

CYNTHIA

Knock knock? May we come in? Just for a moment? Is it all right?

HARRY

Come on in.

CYNTHIA

Don't let us bother you. But I wanted to see the pantry again. You see, years and years ago, when dear Mrs. Rosen and her husband were still alive, and I was a very young thing, I made a long stay with them. And some of my favorite times were spent here in the pantry and even back in the servants quarters.

HARRY

Yeah?

DEXTER

Must have been fun.

CYNTHIA

Heaven. Daddy was painting her portrait, and he couldn't get it right, couldn't get it right, couldn't get it right, but really it was all right: We got along famously. I kept telling him to make her eyes even squiffier so we'd have to stay on to fix them again.

DEXTER

I'll bet you did.

HARRY [struck]

I remember you.

CYNTHIA

I thought so. And I remember you. Francis? Rudolf? Joseph?

HARRY

Harry.

CYNTHIA

Harry! Of course! With the family for years. Faithful Francis! I mean Harry! Always announcing the meals, I remember, and fetching drinks, and doing it incomparably well. . . You know whom I *do* remember? But not his name. That big, strapping chauffeur Mrs. Rosen doted on. I can see his face still, the brutal planes of it—so avid and masterful in his tight coat—and those jodhpurs.

DEXTER

Really!

CYNTHIA [huskily]

Quite the man for that great Cadillac of hers. So kind, he drove me every place I wished to go, day and night.

HARRY

That was—

CYNTHIA

Don't tell me, it's stupid to forget names, and I refuse to have forgotten this one. You see, he made an impression on my virgin heart.

DEXTER

A crush?

CYNTHIA

My secret's out. The tiniest crush, with the nostalgic scent now of violets. Not jealous, are you, dear?

DEXTER
We all have our pasts.

CYNTHIA
Broad-shouldered, not what you'd call refined, but capable, even knowing, in an unschooled, animalistic—

HARRY
That was—

CYNTHIA
No, I insist, don't tell me, it's on the tip of my tongue, the name of that brute—

HARRY
—me.

CYNTHIA
I don't think so.

HARRY
I was chauffeur till Freddie the butler retired and the old lady decided to save a salary by having me do both.

CYNTHIA
No, no, the man I mean *glistened*.

[HARRY has recourse to his glass.]

Oh!

DEXTER
What's going on here?

CYNTHIA

My memory's like a sieve. Of course all this time I'm thinking of that dear driver of Mrs. Biltmore's out on Long Island, another person entirely, so grandfatherly and sweet.

[to DEXTER]

Come, dear.

HARRY

I remember you.

CYNTHIA

Impossible, I'm afraid.

[to DEXTER, leading HIM off]

Daddy gave Mrs. Biltmore skin the color of eggplant. She was not pleased, but so touchingly determined to be modern.

HARRY

Yeah, we had us a time.

[CYNTHIA stops.]

Not that you were the only one. Rich girls, excited by the uniform, the forbidden thrill of servants quarters, were a type not unknown to us in my line of work. Always very practical, protection in their purses. Mostly they fade into each other — but you I remember.

DEXTER

Look here, my man!

HARRY

Your firm young flesh—

DEXTER

Cynthia!

HARRY

Strange to think back, how your body tortured me with some secret I had to find.

CYNTHIA

You were married.

HARRY

Still am.

CYNTHIA

With a little boy.

[MAGGIE enters left, eating caviar, BOBBY following with sandwich tray.]

MAGGIE

Harry, the caviar this year tastes like— Oh, hello.

CYNTHIA [appraising Bobby]

Your son's not very like, I'm afraid, although I'm sure he has many fine qualities. Certainly a youthful thirty-five.

BOBBY

Who's thirty-five? I'm seventeen!

[Exits right.]

                    HARRY
Not ours.

                    MAGGIE
Hah!

                    CYNTHIA
Oh!

                    HARRY
Ours died not much later.

                    MAGGIE
Still a baby.

                    CYNTHIA
I'm sorry.

                    HARRY [indicating CYNTHIA]
Her father was the guy did Mrs. Rosen's picture.

                    MAGGIE
Hah! Not for one minute did she look like that bag lady your father painted. Don't know what he was trying to do, but—

                    CYNTHIA
He was trying to survive. Daddy splashed it on for self-preservation, jungles of color he had to machete his way through with a palette knife. His old women posed with intensity, temples to perfection in jewels and silks and powder, holding their mouths firm, careful not to jiggle their wattles. Their concentration made him very, very nervous. That's why gelatinous green cross-hatchings were the usual result.

MAGGIE
Told the old lady she should have got her money back.

CYNTHIA
Of course. Well, high time we returned to the party.

MAGGIE
One moment, if you please.

CYNTHIA
Really, I hear my name being called —

MAGGIE
If I may —

DEXTER [to CYNTHIA]
We'd better.

CYNTHIA
Yes, well, all right. *Dite.*

MAGGIE
Don't know how to say this — but that summer you and Harry played around, it marked a turning point for us.

CYNTHIA
Look, I'm sorry, but I was all of eighteen or something. The young love power, and youth's a good excuse for using it.

MAGGIE
Harry was never the same man again. Don't know how you did it.

CYNTHIA
Yes?

HARRY

There was hell to pay.

CYNTHIA

Oh?

HARRY

She confronted me, dangling a rubber—

DEXTER

I say!

MAGGIE

He turned a new leaf. Things got better. Not perfect—but hey. You were the last of his girls. So thanks.

CYNTHIA

You're welcome, I'm sure. You're a good woman.

MAGGIE

Thank you.

CYNTHIA

A tolerant woman.

MAGGIE

Thank you. So you want him now, go ahead. Only saving me work.

CYNTHIA

Oh no—

[MAGGIE exits left.]

DEXTER
I say!

HARRY
That's an invite I won't refuse.

DEXTER
I believe the invitation was to the lady.

CYNTHIA
Dexter, be a dear and stuff it. Harry, your wife is remarkable.

HARRY
She is that, Miss— What do I call you?

CYNTHIA
I am the Contessa Thalassa. Cynthia will do.

HARRY [licking lips]
Cynthia. That's it.

CYNTHIA
Dexter dear, go make an appearance out by the punch.

DEXTER
And do what?

CYNTHIA
Sip it and look happy.

DEXTER
Which bowl is spiked?

HARRY
They're both spiked. Tradition.

DEXTER

Cynthia—

CYNTHIA

Beat it, Dexter.

DEXTER

I see where this is heading, and I warn you, get out now. Walk out through the guests and across the lawn, call for the car, meet offers of assistance with a shake of the head, and flee!

CYNTHIA

Go nibble some caviar or something.

DEXTER

And leave you with the help?

CYNTHIA

Vitality is where you find it.

DEXTER

Ignore my advice at your own risk.

CYNTHIA

Risk lies more in what I do, I believe, than in what I ignore.

DEXTER [to HARRY]

How would you feel if I went after *your* wife?

HARRY

Safe.

[DEXTER exits right.]

CYNTHIA

Well. Sorry. Dexter associates marriage with property, so he panics. Not for him the gooey, germy stuff of life. But everything has a time and place, and ours was long ago.

HARRY

Cynthia. . . So how have things gone with you?

CYNTHIA

I've come up in the world. You knew me as the daughter of a titled but impecunious painter who eked out a living by taking longer to paint the faces of society queens than Scheherazade took to weave—whatever it was she never wove. He perfected their wrinkles, analyzed the peculiar inelasticity of dowager skin, shoveled in the free meals, added to a traveling store of canned goods, and presented them with pictures they liked only when critics came to praise. Not an easy life.

HARRY

Do you paint?

CYNTHIA

I go in more for the plastic arts: what you touch, what you mold. They're more dangerous.

HARRY

What happened to him? Old drunk, wasn't he?

CYNTHIA

Father died halfway through his picture of Mrs. Montmorency. Her dewlaps finished him. It was quite sudden.

HARRY

Must have been tough on you.

CYNTHIA
I put his coffin on the *Queen Mary* and wandered by the Whatsit Club and cried buckets. Everyone crowded round, and by some instinct I thinned the herd till, come dawn, I was in the passenger seat of the Jessup boy's Jaguar, flashing a cigar band this way and that on my finger. In due course the cigar band was replaced by gold, the bucket seat by a mansion, my name by his, and his by another's.

HARRY
Dexter's?

CYNTHIA
Among others. He's afraid of you, I think.

HARRY
Is that what he is?

CYNTHIA
Now, now. He's rich and important. He'll tide me over.

HARRY
Then?

CYNTHIA
One thing I don't do is terrify myself by worrying about some time that's yet to arrive. I mean, how silly. Sufficient unto the day. But I am a confident person. Never met the moment I couldn't master.

HARRY
Proud boast.

CYNTHIA

Most people live on a kind of time-line that's like a street. There, they say,

> [points]

that's where I was born (how small and quaint it looks!) and there, at the future end,

> [points]

that's when I shall surely be dead, so I — say most people — estimate myself to be — yes, stretched out, tied down, just about, say —

> [nods]

here or so. Yes. And so that

> [points]

is fading, can be disregarded, and this

> [points]

scares me too much to think about, but

> [nodding]

yes, *this* I can deal with, this point I can whittle down until it's so infinitesimal as to menace no one, not even most people. Most people, Harry, lie down and submit, convinced they're not afraid even as they terrify themselves gazing into the abyss.

HARRY
Were you always like this?

CYNTHIA
I on the other hand take that ribbon of time,

> [backs into storage pantry,
> wraps curtains around
> HERSELF]

wrap it around my hands, look up to heaven, kick the bucking bronco and enjoy the ride.

> [Poses triumphantly.]

Sometimes there are spills — occasionally thrills.

HARRY
Christ, where do you get the energy?

CYNTHIA
Do I make you feel young again?

HARRY
You make me feel old. What's time done to me?

CYNTHIA
Time's a brute. But I see you at the wheel of one of your splendid motors — not with a tea tray in your hands. That's part of it. And I? How's time treated me?

HARRY
With rubber hoses. Not a mark on you.

CYNTHIA
Not all sagging down toward the grave, toward some horizontal equilibrium?

HARRY
Horizontal was always your best angle.

CYNTHIA
You do remember! I was afraid you'd forgotten.

HARRY
I have.

CYNTHIA
Not gallant, are you?

HARRY
Memory fades.

CYNTHIA
Perhaps. But sex stays vivid. In time everything else loses definition, merges into the great fudge. But sex stays vivid.

HARRY
Shhh.

CYNTHIA
Ironic, isn't it? Sex is the great undefiner. Sex takes a moment and focuses on its give-it-to-me aspect, subjects everything to *give-it-to-me*, takes one moment and makes it *huge*.

HARRY
You remember every moment?

CYNTHIA

Or no moments. In sex as in dreams, memory lags. It can't keep up with something so alive. Memory feeds on the carrion of life, the half-done, half-experienced daily grind.

HARRY

You're a wonder, Cynthia. To think I knew you when you had to cadge a place to stay, food to eat—

CYNTHIA

Rest assured, I now possess the obligatory wherewithal. Even went in for a title—chic, in an old-fashioned kind of way.

HARRY

Kids?

CYNTHIA

Only Dexter.

HARRY

You must be a walking scandal.

CYNTHIA

Scandal is merely sex's dry regretful shadow, and I don't care who steps on my shadow. A certain lubriciousness keeps the parts moving. Only if you mark the days to death does it hurt and ache and make you tired and generally strike you as not worth the trouble. If you live by a principle of vitality, scandal poses no threat at all.

HARRY

By God, I admire that.

CYNTHIA
Life is filling yourself up! I've been filling myself up for it seems like centuries, yet I'm as empty as when I started.

HARRY
Me too. Gave it all away.

CYNTHIA
So tell me. I need to know: Why was I your last girl? Was it that bad? Or was it perhaps — sacred? That would be so very sweet. And I like to be nice to those who are nice to me.

[BOBBY enters right at a run.]

BOBBY
More punch! More napkins!

[to CYNTHIA]

Your husband's dunking his head in a punchbowl!

HARRY
Napkins over there.

[BOBBY grabs napkins, HARRY hands pitcher.]

CYNTHIA
Be a dear and help Dexter, won't you — What's his name?

HARRY
Bobby.

CYNTHIA
—Bobby? Lead him some place where he can pout without disturbing the other guests.

BOBBY
Yes, ma'am.

[Exits right.]

HARRY
We maybe should get out there.

CYNTHIA
What do you say, Harry: Go in the garage, find a backseat? An empty maid's room? Or a closed-off bedroom in the west wing? Let's feed that desire one never loses, for to lose it is to lose life itself. Later I'll go back to the party, hair mussed, lips squashed, with a distant air and wide-pupiled eyes, my trademark crispness softened, and a wisp of straw or something on my shoulder. Return to the punchbowl, a new chapter suspected, my legend burnished—

HARRY
I can't.

CYNTHIA
But Bobby looks as though he could dole out the punch for *hours*.

HARRY
If you want, we could take a bottle and disappear. Appearances will satisfy me. I'm an old man, Cynthia.

CYNTHIA
Don't you want more than that?

HARRY

Maggie would kill me.

CYNTHIA

Seems more likely to congratulate you.

HARRY

I would be derelict in my duties.

CYNTHIA

Everyone knows butlers uncork more than champagne.

HARRY

It would present a sorry example to Bobby.

CYNTHIA

You'll give him a chance to shine in your absence, and a rare clue to what it is to be a man. Oh, how delicious to play with desire like this.

[Embraces HIM. Carrying tray, MAGGIE crosses from left to right.]

MAGGIE

At your age. Well, if you can. But they'll need more punch soon.

[HARRY breaks away, frenziedly opens Champagne bottles: *Pop! Pop! Pop! Pop! Pop! Pop! Pop! Pop!*
MAGGIE briefly looks in during the popping.]

                        CYNTHIA
But how to begin? Perhaps if I close my eyes—

                        [closes eyes]

Oh yes, that's right.

                        [brushes HARRY's front]

You just do it.

                        HARRY [attentive]
The old urge.

                        CYNTHIA
Older than the hills, like me—

                        HARRY [backing up]
Didn't mean that—

                        CYNTHIA [stalking HIM around
                             table]
Oh, but I'm more than old, I go back to the age of the gods. That lovely feeling of being ancient? Everything dried out, beyond question, only bone structure left behind, that skeleton we bequeath the future as our final summation—bones that resist time, yet lie scattered, ripe for the taking. So vulnerable. Oh, this so reminds me of that first time. Remember, Harry? For days everywhere I turned, your arm barred my way. When I gasped for air, I got your kisses. When I flew through the glades, you nipped at my heels. When I ate, you fed me. Before I slept, you smoothed the sheets. When I woke up, you brought in the breakfast tray. My downfall was that breakfast tray. Where your wife was during that time—

HARRY
Taking care of the baby like I should have.

CYNTHIA
That's right, its illness tied her down, gave you the freedom to pursue me—

HARRY
And catch you.

CYNTHIA [catching HIM]
You pinned back the butterfly's wings on a Sunday morning, no one around, in a bedstead of ancient worm-eaten walnut.

HARRY [bucking and kicking]
You bucked, you kicked—

CYNTHIA [letting go]
And couldn't get free. We brought out from behind cloth the flesh in question—so unexpected and interesting—and played the sheer brute wonderful facts of power and wet pleasures to the finish, then covered up decently again.

HARRY
I made a woman of you—

CYNTHIA
Or a man. Your embraces slammed me like a printing press slams paper, replicated themselves backwards, made me an etching of conquest to be hung among others. You nailed your trophy to the wall, and closed it on our sacred chapter. Or was it sacred?

HARRY
It's the chase that's the thing. Any man can tell you that.

CYNTHIA
"The thing." That's too neat, too beginning, middle and end. It's not the chase, or the end of the chase, it's the swim in the current of sex, senses stimulated, looking at life to see it as it is then, a tangle of limbs and complications and pleasures, connections, confusions, needs and amnesia and urgency. Life set out not cold and gray for study purposes, but pulsing with a semblance to itself, a study for *living* purposes. Oh, to wrap yourself in that moment— Oh, Harry, you owe me—

> [BOBBY enters right. HARRY leaps away from CYNTHIA.]

BOBBY
More finger sandwiches!

> [Grabs tray, exits right.]

HARRY
Cynthia, we have our memories, and it's better that way—

CYNTHIA
Life's so short. Why wallow in memories? Harry, haven't you learned we must live in the here and the now and the altogether—

> [Stepping out of jumpsuit, backs HARRY up to curtains.]

Take me. I feel nostalgic. I'll make a man out of you.

HARRY
More to it than that. More complicated than you say.

CYNTHIA

But it's so simple. In different times, different places, I disappear, gone save for a puddle of clothing left behind. Take me, Harry.

[Backs HIM into through curtains.]

HARRY

No, I tell you. They need me at the punchbowl!

CYNTHIA

Give it to me, Harry!

[Backs HIM out of sight.]

Give it to me! Give it to me! *Give it to me!*

[HARRY screams.]

[BLACKOUT]

[END OF PLAY]

AND OTHER PLAYS AND ADAPTATIONS –

Seductions of a Wedding Night

A Comedy in Three Scenes

Seductions of a Wedding Night

CAST OF CHARACTERS

JASON, a student, 20.

DAN, a New Yorker, 40.

SCENE AND TIME

Motel room in Iowa, before and after a wedding, and the next morning. Two beds face TV set. Door, closet, bathroom left, window right.

SCENE ONE

AT RISE, DAN is sleeping. Open suitcase on other bed. Telephone rings.

                    DAN

Hello. . .? Oh, hi. . . That's OK, should get moving, must be getting time. . . Wondered about that, Scott's wedding night, his best man can't expect to stay with him. . . Sure, there's an extra bed, send him over. . . No imposition at all, he seemed nice. . . Bye.

              [Hangs up.]

Hey, anything for my nephew's best friend.

             [Smooths hair, tucks shirt in, moves suitcase to floor, smooths beds, opens curtains to sunshine.
               Knock. DAN opens door to JASON in shorts, sneakers, T shirt, carrying bag.]

Hey, Jason? I'm Dan, Scott's uncle. We met at the rehearsal dinner.

                    JASON

Yeah, I remember. Nice of you to put me up.

DAN

No problem. Three's a crowd on a wedding night, or so they say.

JASON

Somehow didn't hit me before. Scott and I have been running around like crazy since we flew in.

DAN

That bed okay?

JASON

Sure.

> [Sits on bed, watching DAN lay out a suit.]

DAN

Should think about getting over there. You should be early in case you have to soothe the groom.

JASON

I can't believe it, my best friend is getting married.

DAN

Pretty amazing.

JASON

Are you married?

DAN [holding up two ties]

Me? Married? *I am not going to ask if he has a girlfriend.* No, I'm the gay uncle.

> [Decides on tie. JASON reaches
> to the other.]

JASON
That's cool. What a great tie.

> [DAN lays JASON's choice on
> suit. JASON puts on
> sunglasses.]

DAN
Are you missing classes for this?

JASON
A few, but it's worth it.

DAN
So you up on your duties as best man?

JASON
Well, we had the rehearsal. I'm pretty vague on it, though.

DAN
Thank God I'm here to show you the ropes! I've been best man for my other brother — twice.

JASON
Yeah?

DAN
The best man's crucial — far more important than people realize — but the comforting thing is, no one will see you. Everyone's looking at the bride and groom. First, it's your job to get Scott to the ceremony. Groom traditionally tries to back out.

JASON [seriously]
All right.

DAN
Lock the doors and hide the liquor.

JASON
Scott doesn't drink.

DAN
You never know. That's job one.

JASON [smiling]
Right.

DAN
Job two is you produce the bride's ring and hand it to the groom so he can put it on her finger.

JASON
They mentioned that.

DAN
Before the ceremony, I suggest you slip it on your pinky so you won't have to scrounge for it.

JASON
Good idea.

DAN
And at the reception you have to propose the first toast. Sometimes you have to fight for the privilege. At my brother's latest, the bride's father had plans of his own, and I had to insist in a most unpleasant manner that I go first.

JASON
What did you say?

DAN
That I'd break his legs —

JASON
I mean for the toast.

DAN
Oh, something short and sincere.

JASON
Should I prepare beforehand?

DAN
Whatever makes you more comfortable.

[JASON looks out window.]

Lord, you have an arresting face. May simply be your season of bloom, but we're talking major bloom. I think, while you're looking out the window, one little glance at your legs.

[Turns, looks.]

Oh God I'm hard.

JASON
Look how the fields fold into each other. So pretty.

DAN
Umm.

[JASON gets camera, snaps picture through window.]

I could fall in love with you without even trying. No, I won't fall in love with you. You're twenty — nineteen maybe. You're straight. If you're not straight — and maybe you're not — you're still twenty, vulnerable, in a fog, not a free agent. Maybe you could be had, but you couldn't give yourself in any meaningful, free way, in any way that would do me *any good. Except. . . Listen, Danny me boy, when you meet your lifetime lover, you'll tell yourself falling in love is inadvisable — and you'll be wrong.*

[JASON snaps picture of DAN.]

DAN
Hey, no fair. Had my landscape face on.

JASON [nudging DAN]
Look at the cows. They're just waiting. I wonder what for?

DAN
Mmm. *And silos stand against the barns like erections. The world unveils its sexual nature when you share a motel room in Iowa.*

[JASON steps back, camera poised, and waits.]

No, I won't seduce you. Want to, but you're my nephew's friend. In some absurd measure, my hospitality must be a sacred trust. Dammit, dammit, dammit.

[Turns ruefully from window.]

JASON [snapping]
Gotcha!

DAN
Hey!

JASON
So when do I toast?

DAN
You'll know. An atmosphere descends. You'll sense it. Just go ahead and do it. It'll come naturally.

JASON
I guess we'll really party tonight.

DAN
How old are you, Jason?

JASON
Twenty. Scott says you live in New York?

DAN
That I do.

JASON
Neat. I'd love to see Greenwich Village.

DAN
It's nice.

JASON
You're a writer?

DAN
That I am, not that I make a living at it.

JASON

Are you working on anything now?

DAN

A new story.

JASON

What's it about?

DAN

Tell him. Bring everything to the surface. A seductive little tale with lots of naked male flesh. It's at too early a stage. Bad karma to talk about work in progress.

JASON

That's cool. Mind if I shower first?

DAN

Go ahead.

[JASON exits with bag.]

Coward.

[BLACKOUT]

[END OF SCENE ONE]

SCENE TWO

AT RISE, curtains drawn against darkness, JASON crouches at TV wearing only gym shorts.
    Enter DAN, tie loosened.

JASON
Thought you were coming right back.

DAN
Thought you'd be sound asleep. One last drink with everybody.

> [Sits on bed, takes off shoes.]

What a day. Well, the deed is done and bride and groom are off to wherever. Did you have fun?

JASON
After I got over my jitters.

> [Sits next to DAN.]

Did I look nervous?

DAN
Not a bit. You did great.

> [Gets up, takes off jacket and shirt, revealing undershirt.]

And you got him there on time.

JASON
Can't believe my best friend's married.

DAN
Yep, the ring's in his nose now. Speaking of rings, you handled it well.

JASON
Did you see, he had trouble with it?

DAN [taking off undershirt]
Kind of sexy watching him push it down her finger.

JASON
I am so tired, just want to crash and sleep right through. Been going for days. Scott and I saw the sunrise this morning.

DAN
That's always fun.

JASON
And the night before was frat rush.

[Closes eyes.]

Might take a forklift to move me. I am wiped out.

[DAN goes off. JASON goes back to fiddling with TV. Toilet flushes, off.]

Nothing on TV. Can't even find the game scores.

[DAN enters, stripped to shorts, and goes up to JASON, who stands up straight. DAN embraces and kisses HIM. JASON responds.]

DAN
I've wanted to do that since we met.

JASON
And I've been waiting.

DAN
I had scruples? Thank God a few drinks makes things clearer.

[BLACKOUT.
LIGHTS BURST ON as JASON fiddles with TV. Toilet flushes off.]

JASON
Nothing on TV. Can't even find the game scores.

[DAN enters, stripped to shorts, and gets into bed. JASON gets into other bed. DAN turns bedside lamp OFF and flips through channels with remote mounted on table between beds.]

DAN
He's twenty, he's legal. There's a remote.

JASON

Yeah?

DAN

But they glued it down.

JASON

They don't want their remote to go remote.

DAN

You can take control.

JASON

You keep it. Nothing on. Wait: that's their new video.

[Violent colors bathe THEM.]

DAN

Don't think: Do. Now's the time. Hop over with a smile. Do it! Now! The moment has arrived! Ready, set: Go! One, Two, Three: Go!

JASON

I better get to sleep. Have to read *Plato's Republic* by Monday.

DAN

Won't you have time tomorrow?

JASON

Maybe on the plane. But tomorrow night my frat chooses new pledges.

DAN

Yeah, do you get to blackball 'em?

JASON
I hate that. Two balls to reject them. I hate it when someone says, I don't know, I didn't like him much. Christ! It takes all kinds. But everyone ends up balling everyone else's friends.

DAN
Oh: Black-balling. What kind of guys do you like?

JASON
We like guys who can talk to anyone. Not too preppy, not too weird. I'm half way between, myself.

DAN
I think Scott's lucky to have you for a best friend.

JASON
Yeah, he's a great guy. You're his favorite uncle.

DAN
I know it. *Come on: Do you want an engraved invitation? How can I be gay if I'm not predatory? Get over there. The worst that can happen is he'll say no.* Their videos are better than their music.

JASON
Did you see their last one? With the matador?

DAN
One, Two, Three: Go! Go for it. . . ! Do it, for God's sake! Do it! Do it! Do it. . . ! No, I missed it.

JASON
Never saw such tight pants. Goodnight.

DAN [hitting remote OFF button]
Goodnight.

— A JOURNAL OF THE PLAGUE YEAR,

[BLACKOUT.
LIGHTS GO UP HALF.
TV's on. JASON, in HIS bed, has back to DAN's empty bed.
Toilet flushes off. DAN enters, stripped to shorts, gets in HIS bed, turns off lamp and TV.]

DAN

Why must it be pursuit and flight, a winner and a loser, one getting it, the other brought to ground? I suppose youth has to wait for someone to pounce so as to maintain innocence, or its technical definition... Hey, it's my room, right? If I make a move, goes with the territory, right...? Real attractive, Dan. But twenty's old enough to watch out for himself. You like him. Worst that can happen is he'll say no... Who are you kidding? The worst would be if he said yes. A one-night stand. A notch in your bedpost earned by satisfying his curiosity. In the morning he'll have forgotten, or pretend he has. I'd feel real pain if I had him once and never again... Ah, fuck it. Trust instinct. Jason? Jason?

[DAN gets up and slips into JASON's bed. JASON turns and THEY kiss.]

JASON

Dan, I've never done this before. I'm scared.

DAN

Don't be. I'm right here.

[THEY kiss.]

JASON
This is wonderful. I was hoping...

[THEY kiss. DAN goes rigid.]

DAN
Oh God! He's just a kid. This is wrong. And I've got an early flight.

JASON
What's the matter?

DAN
I can't do this, Jason! I'm sorry. You don't want it this way.

JASON
Why not?

DAN
Seduced? Your youth and inexperience taken advantage of by an older man? That's not how it should be. Should be mutual, a sharing and giving from a standpoint of equality, a coming together —

JASON
I like you, Dan. I want you.

DAN
Experience of a piece with the cheapness of a motel room? Slam-bam expectation, born of slam-bam convention?

JASON
Are you all right?

DAN
I've been in love. Intimacy's too serious a thing to —

JASON

Lighten up: I don't want to get intimate—just physical.

DAN

Ah. Whereas I need connection. Which a day's acquaintance can't provide.

JASON

You're weird.

DAN

Better weird than made a sacrifice to your youth and beauty, hung out to dry on your sturdy questing limbs.

JASON

I said yes.

DAN

Maybe you're so young *No* comes out *Yes?* You say *Yes,* but endure me through nausea, or—worse—as flesh and not as me.

JASON

I can watch out for myself. I'm starting my junior year.

DAN

Your *No* I could trust. *No* would be perfectly credible.

JASON

I said yes.

DAN

This gives me some of that feeling of pain and waste that happens when love ends. I'm sorry, Jason. Forgive me.

>   [Goes back to HIS bed.
>   BLACKOUT.
>   LIGHTS GO UP HALF,
>   EACH in own bed, lamp and
>   TV off.]

>   JASON

Goodnight.

>   DAN

Goodnight. *You have a responsibility here. Think how lost he feels, needing help to turn desire into sex — and all you're doing is behaving like a gentleman... You're full of shit. Besides, it's too late... No, it's not too late. Use your verbal gift, that gift of gab. Give him a chance. Be direct.*

>   [DAN turns lamp ON. JASON
>   stirs, looks over. DAN glowers
>   at HIM.]

>   JASON

What's the matter?

>   DAN

Nothing.

>   JASON

What?

>   DAN

I can't sleep.

>   JASON [turning away]

I'm really tired, you know?

                    DAN

Sorry.

                    [Turns lamp OFF.]

You idiot. Bastard. Dan, you are the dumbest —

                    [JASON turns lamp ON, looks
                    at DAN.]

                    JASON

Dan? Danny, I can't sleep.

                    DAN

Me neither.

                    JASON

Too strung up, I guess. What with the wedding and all.

                    DAN

Yeah. Excited.

                    JASON

Need to come down.

                    DAN

Relax.

                    JASON

Know what helps?

                    DAN

Hot milk?

                    JASON

Massage.

                    DAN

That's true.

                    JASON

Do you like massage?

                    DAN

Love it.

                    JASON

I'll do you if you'll do me.

                    DAN

Sounds fair.

                    [JASON gets on DAN's bed,
                    straddles HIM, massages back.
                    LIGHTS GO DOWN
                    GRADUALLY.]

Mmmmmmm.

                    JASON

Does that feel good?

                    DAN

Very.

                    [Goes rigid.]

Hold on: What's going on here? He's seducing me – seducing me into servicing him. We'll do it with never a word between us, no personal basis at all. That's no good. We'd avert our faces in the morning, and he'd put his gay side away for good, and I could never face my nephew again —

JASON
So many knots. What's the matter?

DAN
This isn't working, Jason. Thanks, but let's just go to sleep. Sorry.

[Pulls sheet up. JASON gets
into own bed.
BLACKOUT.
LIGHTS GO UP HALF,
EACH in own bed. DAN props
HIMSELF up and looks over.]

DAN
Whatever I could say, he wouldn't understand. Youth knows only what it wants, what it's entitled to. . . There you go, treating him as less than an individual. Jason knows only what he wants. And he could do better than me. Being gorgeous. . . "You rejected me," he could say, " — pre-emptively rejected me — because I have all the beauty?" "No, no," I would tell him, "I'm proud of my body, I'm in good shape, and at forty I've learned a thing or two. I'm glad I'm forty and not twenty. You'd be lucky to be with me, if the circumstances were right. But they're wrong. . ."

Come on, Dan: Lying here burning with lust and doing nothing about it is self-betrayal. Being out of the closet means staying out! What keeps me in my own bed must be a remnant of my own homophobia, some unredeemed trace of disgust at sex between men. Dan, you owe it to your manhood — Dammit, you owe it to the gay community!

[Leaps up, shakes JASON
awake.]

Jason!

                    JASON
What is it? What do you want?

            [DAN smiles wickedly, touches
            JASON.]

What are you doing? I can't believe this.

                    DAN
Believe it. You know what I want. You want it too.

            [JASON jumps out of bed,
            DAN pursuing.]

                    JASON
What I want's a night's sleep. I thought you were a nice guy—

                    DAN
Not only nice, but *good*.

                    JASON
One more step and I get the management.

                    DAN
How sordid.

                    JASON
You're sordid!

                    DAN
Don't you want it?

                    JASON
No! We only just met—

DAN

It's that?

JASON

I'm straight, you know.

DAN

What are you doing sending out mixed signals if you're so straight?

JASON

That's my privilege. I'm only twenty years old.

DAN

Okay, I'm very, very sorry. Kiss me.

[Leaps into JASON's bed.
JASON runs off.]

Yes! Oh yeah, Jason, this is it. The delight of young beauty, all potential, yet actual, affectionate, responsive in the here and now. Of skin and— Oh God, oh God. Jason, I think I love you.

[LIGHTS GO DOWN
GRADUALLY.]

Come on, Jason, come back to bed. I want to be decent. I want to be decent, and also to get it on. Instinct impels me—

[Yawns.]

But instinct's as tired as I am. Instinct says, go to sleep. One, Two, Three: Go!

[BLACKOUT]

Coward.

> [LIGHTS GO UP HALF on
> DAN and JASON in bed
> together, DAN's face averted.]

> JASON

That's all right, I've read about it in books. Apparently it happens sometimes.

> [BLACKOUT.
> LIGHTS GO UP HALF,
> DAN in JASON's bed, JASON
> in DAN's.
> JASON rises on his elbow
> and studies DAN sleeping.]

> JASON

What am I, chopped liver? I'm ready to party, I tell you so, accidentally bump your knee at the reception, more than once, give you my most flattering attention, tag along after you — and you go right to sleep like an old man? I'm good-looking. Good body. Young. Friendly. Don't I rate a roll in the hay in Iowa?

> DAN [waking up]

To be thrown into a set-up like this with someone so cute and sweet and virginal, and my nephew's best friend. . . I have to show restraint. Self-respect and my own capacity for pain demand it, but it's best for you too, Jason, I'm sure of it. Practically sure of it.

> JASON

I don't get it. Are you that old?

DAN
Forty isn't thirty, and it sure isn't twenty. Maybe it's the fear of rejection? But also fear of acceptance. If I were another kid your age, the potential for damage wouldn't be there. But to be older, the seducer — that's taking on a lot.

JASON
I'm insulted. Rejecting me is your power trip. We could be having fun.

DAN
But to what purpose? Assume you don't freak out when I actually touch you, where could it go? By a fluke we're sharing a room tonight. Our lives have nothing to do with each other. We live a thousand miles apart. We'd only be using each other like pieces of meat.

JASON
Pieces of meat? I like the way you put it. Sounds sexy.

> [Reaches over. DAN shrinks from HIS touch.]

DAN
See? That scares me. If I'd picked you up hitchhiking, maybe I'd be in blow-job heaven right about now. If we were strangers. . . But Scott's friendship makes you a person to me. And I don't want to be a stranger in the dark to you, stripped of individuality.

JASON
Even if we're stripped of everything?

DAN
There's torment in it whatever I do. Must be coming across as a wimp. But look what you're doing: By leaving the initiative to me, you abdicate responsibility for yourself, put your sexuality at a remove from yourself, and impose guilt on me. That's not healthy.

JASON
I'm supposed to come on to you so you have nothing to feel guilty about?

DAN
You'd do better meeting some kid at school. Unless it's something you want to try *away* from school?

JASON
I live in a frat house. I date girls. Everyone knows who the campus fags are. Gross old men sometimes lick their lips at me or make kissing sounds. How can I find somebody nice without risking everything? I hope I never get as old as you. Excuse me if I take back my own solitary bed.

[THEY warily exchange beds.]

Good night.

DAN
Good night.

[THEY lie with backs to EACH OTHER. LIGHTS GO DOWN GRADUALLY.
JASON props HIMSELF up on elbow and looks steadily over at DAN.]

– *A JOURNAL OF THE PLAGUE YEAR,*

[BLACKOUT]

[END OF SCENE TWO]

SCENE THREE

AT RISE, sunlight streams in. Sound of shower, off. DAN stands in shorts, shirt, socks, combing HIS wet hair.

DAN
You haven't always hesitated. Do you decline the mercies of a very young man to your aging body? I'm in shape. Even if my ass drops daily and my love handles swell.

> [Pulls out front of shorts.
> Shower stops.]

My cock looks like menace and strength. Anyone would say so. No, I look okay, considering. Let a young man take me if he wants.

> [Gets dressed. Enter JASON, dressed, hair wet, manner distant.]

JASON
You should get going.

DAN
Yeah. How'd you sleep?

JASON
Great.

DAN

I'll be at Scott's parents' for Christmas. The newlyweds will be there.

JASON

I'll be around too.

DAN

See you then, then.

[THEY shake hands.]

JASON

Thanks for putting me up.

DAN

Any time.

[Exits with suitcase. Putting on eyeglasses, JASON packs bag. Looks up with surprise as DAN knocks, enters, takes pad from pocket, scribbles.]

JASON

Hey!

DAN

Wear glasses, do you? Too insecure to let me see? Silly. You couldn't be cuter.

[Tears paper from pad.]

Almost forgot, here's my phone number and address. If you come to New York—to Greenwich Village—I have a couch.

                    JASON

I'm in school.

                    DAN

Well, but any time.

                    JASON [takes paper, grimacing]

Thanks.

            [THEY shake hands again.
            JASON turns to HIS bag.]

                    DAN

Pitiful, right? To let you know there's a lech in New York waiting for you. But it's the best I can do. It is a far, far better thing that I did than I have done in a while. But you would not have made me happy, Jason. Except for one night. For one glorious night you'd have put me in heaven. Damn!

            [Exits.]

            [BLACKOUT]

            [END OF PLAY]

– *A JOURNAL OF THE PLAGUE YEAR,*

AND OTHER PLAYS AND ADAPTATIONS –

Chocolate Meringue Pie

A Comic Monologue

Chocolate Meringue Pie

CHARACTER

VIOLET, a strong woman, mid-50s, in flowered housedress and white sneakers.

SCENE AND TIME

Yard of green suburban tract house, a weekday in April. Sun moves from one side to the other during the play.

AT RISE, VIOLET comes outdoors to wave goodbye to car heard driving off. Light's angle tells us it's perhaps 8:00 a.m.
   Door closes.

                    VIOLET
I'll be fine, Doris. Lots to do. See you after school, kids! Learn a lot!

           [Ambles around looking at
           plants.]

These plants are like this family: hardly out of the bulb stage. Everything they need packed in a lumpen package just waiting for water and sun. Touching.

           [Stoops, touches plant.]

I love this tender green of first growth, a shoot offered to the air and sun. The darker, confident green of growth added to growth doesn't move me as this first thin green, spun in pure hope out of inner resources, moves me.

           [Pokes flower bed.]

Nursery tags poking up, declarations that someday this earth shall be— what?

           [Reads tag.]

Irises. Pretty.

> [Surveys yard, then with air of having things to do goes to door. Cannot open it.]

My land.

> [Takes handkerchief from sleeve, blows nose, tries again.]

My land. It's locked.

> [Searches SELF for key. Looks under mat. Feels top of door frame. Looks in mailbox. Walks away, regarding door and blowing nose.]

My land.

> [Pokes flower bed.]

Gladiolas. Well, they're nice, too. If you like funerals. How could I come outside without the key Doris gave me?

> [Circles. Searches frame and mat again. Cups hands on window.]

There's your room, Violet—yours for good if you agree to make your visit permanent. Its own bathroom. Own television.

> [Turns.]

View of your step-grandchildren playing.

> [Looks inside.]

And there's your key. Right where you left it—as usual. At least you made your bed—pushed the pull-out couch back in. Wish I had that knitting. Came outdoors to look at the plants. A normal suburban activity, I'm sure. And now I'm an interloper in a homemade dress, embarked on a day out on her son's lawn in April.

> [Ambles, admiring flower
> beds.]

So this is suburbia. Surely a land austere as any my great-grandfather crossed in his covered wagon. And about as friendly as Indian Country when the wars were on. Doris and Jimmy are addicted to these places. There was that house near New York, very like this. And that one outside Atlanta. What color was it—peach? I wonder if they'll ever graduate to a house someone else has lived in before. But we love our far suburban frontier.

> [Tries door again.]

Never lock my own door. I'm sure I should, though.

> [Rings bell, holds breath, looks
> at neighbors' houses.]

Who lives here? Sons and daughters of pioneers? Maybe—Maybe I could knock on someone's door? Oh, Doris might be embarrassed. Don't know who she knows, who she doesn't know. To come home and find me missing, to run outdoors frantically calling "Violet! Violet!" and then see me—to boot—come out of some house she's been shunning—for whatever good reasons—

[Shakes head.]

Can't risk it. Let alone, I can't tell which houses would welcome an old stranger lady. None, most likely. Nothing against them, either. Not like it used to be years ago, when a stranger was someone you were inclined to help because often enough strangers helped you. Nowadays you don't know. Whoever rings your bell could be there to tie you up and ransack you. Suburbia gathers the family safe in the castle against the other families, puts out moats and drawbridges disguised as sidewalks and hedges. Cunning that they camouflage their castles as split-levels, and color them like cartoons.

[Realizes SHE's on neighbor's lawn, skitters towards center.]

Good thing there's a hedge to tell me where my family's land ends. Being careful to stay on it, I will stroll and inspect. If need be, water the flowers.

[Moves hose.]

Ordinary activities around here. Legal, and exactly what a homeowner looking out the window wishes to see the neighbors doing. Building up the neighborhood. . .

They can't spend all day looking out the window. So each neighbor, glancing outside in the course of the day, will have a glimpse of me and never suspect me a locked-out step-grandmother roaming her pasture all day long. If someone sees me this morning, and again this afternoon, I will merely seem—conscientious. . . If I were inside and saw me, I'd park myself by the window and watch. Fill the teapot, bring a plate of cookies. *What is she up to? What on earth is that loony old lady doing? Must be crazy.* I'll stand and wait. Look as though I locked myself out. . . which I did. . . Oh, I can't.

> [Ambles.]

I could leave, walk to—to the library? Leaf through a magazine. Memorize a recipe. Find a phone, call Jimmy at work, precipitate a crisis, eyes rolling ceilingward: "It's my step-mother. An emergency." That's if someone gave me a dime.

> [Checking pocket, finds half
> roll of Life-Savers.]

Life-Savers. Good. Assorted flavors. My favorite. Better ration them, though.

> [Restores Life-Savers to
> pocket.]

Doris pointed out the library to me. That way and that way, then that way. Or that way. I think.

To face facts— As Dad used to say, to face facts: If I missed the library, couldn't find my way back in a thousand years. The green house between a blue house and a yellow one. Green between the blue and the yellow. No, not good enough. Step one foot on the sidewalk and I'm a goner in a pastel wonderland.

Or I could look for the children's school. When I was a little girl, children from the farms would sometimes find their sheepdog pawing at the windows for them, having got away

— A JOURNAL OF THE PLAGUE YEAR,

and sniffed out the route. It was good for an early dismissal. "Take your dog home." "Take your step-grandmother home?" Doubt it.

[Bends to inspect soil close-up.]

Where there's soil, there's always something to see. Boulder size lumps, leaves unfurling, tangles of root, a clean smell of work and growth. I can't be bored. Not I. No, thank you.

[Replaces soil.]

Well, these beds are fine. Time I thought about lunch.

[Catches SELF.]

Oh.

[Makes circuit of lawn.]

Wanted to bake cookies this morning. That younger boy loves my sugar cookies. Can't get enough of them. So simple even a boy can bake them, no failure possible. And boys cannot handle failure. Well, neither can men.

You sift five and a half cups of flour. Why sift it, he asked, and his mother was quick with the answer: *Because.* I told him, you sift it so lightness is baked right in. Three cups sugar, two teaspoons salt, one teaspoon baking soda. Mix in a paper sack. He loves that part. Cut in two cups Crisco and put it aside, in the icebox if you like. Not strictly necessary, it's not dough yet. It's a mix that keeps. When you want to bake up some cookies, take three cups of cookie mix, add one egg, one and a half teaspoons vanilla extract, stir until the dough is smooth and fluffy. Roll it out, then get your cookie cutters, cut out your stars and leaves and hearts and, oh, my, any shape. Bake at three hundred, seventy-five degrees. How long? Till they take on that brown, please-get-us-out-of-here look. Can't say exactly, because baking times vary with altitude and the Navajos live between one and two miles above sea level. Easterners never know that. Around here, I imagine things cook up fast.

My land, I'm hungry.

> [Roots around flowerbed. Pulls up plant, sniffs.]

Scallions! Won't starve, then. If it comes to that. And there's water, although water...

> [Looks longingly towards house.]

No, I can hold out. Never know when you might be locked out, I guess. Haven't felt this dislocated and helpless since— since— No, that makes no sense.

> [Walks.]

No sense whatever. Not even when Jack died last year. But Mother died forty-three years ago.

I was twelve. Hit Dad like a ton of bricks. He didn't meet Lucille for almost ten years after. For me, school all day, housework at night. Cooking. Sewing. Cleaning. Taking care of Dad. Learning what a man likes to eat, how a man likes to live. I was busy. I was learning. Had the energy of youth.

Hit him like a ton of bricks. He worked — taught high school — but at home just sat in his chair with his feet up, reading. In summer, he sat on the porch swing, reading. But he did the heavy spadework in the garden in early spring, turning the earth for the beans and tomatoes that ate up our back yard. Looked so mournful, taking his long-handled spade to that soil. When morning glories bloomed in the hedge he turned up the blossoms with both hands and looked into them with deep, grieving eyes. A very silent man. Men are silent. It must help them. Although I don't see how.

Into the night, Dad sat staring at that close print he preferred. Missed his wife. Never noticed me. But I took pride in keeping him comfortable and well fed and the house clean, shades pulled down to keep an even gloom so the big hulking furniture looked its best. My land, how I worked. All the things Mother taught me. My memories of her come through a dusting of flour from off her grandmother's breadboard.

Of course I had no time for boys. Never felt the lack. I liked boys, and knew some nice ones. Saw them at school and at church, but had no time to see them other times. They did like my baking. Especially my Chocolate Meringue Pie. My famous brainstorm.

[Holds arms out, palms up.]

Fifteen years old, about this time of year. Looked out the window and saw the pear trees engulfed in blossom like Dagwood carrying packages for Blondie. Air was so rich, smelled so good and interesting. I felt — I looked at the garden and then at the cupboard. Sheer inspiration. I know about perspiration, but Chocolate Meringue Pie was sheer one-hundred-percent inspiration. Pulled down what I needed by instinct, mixed exactly what was wanted in the right proportions, not knowing what I was doing, and whipped up a masterpiece. If I do say so. Boys came back for seconds, implored thirds if they thought they could get away with it. Great success. The one year I entered, a long time later, it won the blue ribbon at the New Mexico State Fair.

[Pause.]

A boy has to see a lot of you before he can really, truly like you, for keeps. That's my theory why I was a maiden lady until I was thirty-eight years old. Too busy, too. Went to college right in town, to Muncie Normal. Learned a good deal there. Literature. History. How to handle a classroom of restless children. Came out with a high degree in home economics and the determination to take my talents in running a comfortable, regular, orderly, respectable household someplace where they needed such lore.

Dad didn't say anything. I said, Dad, we're pioneer stock, my blood says to move on, I wouldn't be happy staying in Muncie my whole life, and I have something to give, something they won't get unless I go. Stayed on, though, several more years. Taught elementary grades. Sang in the choir. Filled the cellar with rhubarb and canned beans. Then I applied for a job with the Indian Service, got it, and Dad put me on the train for New Mexico. He didn't say much, but he didn't say no. And things got better for him after he got together with Lucille. She was a good wife to him.

[Stoops over turf.]

Forty-eight years. You never catch up with early deaths.

> [Gets up.]

Well, this lawn's coming along fine, time I thought about lunch.

> [Catches SELF.]

Or not.

> [Takes out Life-Savers, pops one in mouth.]

Lemon. Simply need to muster my strength, dragoon my resources, keep a positive mental attitude, pray against rain, and I will be here when Doris comes home. I'll tell her, Oh, I stepped out to admire your daffodils five minutes ago, door closed behind me.

No, I'll tell her everything. That I have been browsing around the yard like a dumb cow since she left in the morning, right up until she picked up the carpool at school, dropped kids off over the subdivision, and rolled up in front of her own house.

> [Smiles.]

I'm fine. I can handle the rigors of suburbia. The crabgrass won't attack. No packs of rabid dogs roaming, not yet anyway. Weather moderate. It might shower later.

> [Looks at sky.]

I doubt it.

> [Looks longingly after passing car.]

Never can tell when you'll be locked out. You uproot and settle again, are a pioneer in your time, and so on, and then something happens out of your control.

> [Sucks on LifeSaver, squints at sun.]

Can't be too long now. Unless— an accident. If something did happen I could survive the night. Wish I'd thought to put a flannel lining in this dress. Gets cold when the sun goes down. But I'd survive, I imagine. Might be best not to sleep. To keep moving. Could wish for something in the way of lawn furniture. Wouldn't mind sitting down for a spell right now. A folding aluminum thing with scratchy plastic straps. Or anything. Maybe—

> [squints]

Maybe borrow a neighbor's? If I'm very quiet? No. No, find an old lady sitting in your lawn chair, you call the police. An Indiana lady in a red desert Indian reservation would not be stranger, and Lord knows I got looked at in my time. Mind you, no one calls the police on the Indian Service.

Navajos of astonishing dignity and utter silence, exotic icons discreetly staring at *me*. A few scattered white schoolteachers, good for round-robin dinners and shopping expeditions to Gallup. But the Navajo. *Yahehteh.* A great gulf fixed, we used to say. Well, they had their ways, I had mine. Very good students. They learned the secrets of homemaking with reverence. To see a Navajo girl bake blueberry muffins or make a bed with hospital corners or run up striped kitchen curtains gives you a funny feeling, like you are witnessing sacred rituals performed by those more devoted to their inner meaning than you are yourself. True believers. In a hogan the knowledge of how to set the table for a formal dinner party is of dubious utility. Even the Indian Service knew that, on some level. But we gave them a look from the inside at how white people live, to make of it what they would, and I'm sure it was beneficial.

[Scrutinizes grass.]

At least get some weeds up.

[Pulls scant handful of weeds.]

My land, they're baby weeds.

Jack would know what to do. Why, hours ago, he'd have — what? Not broken a window. Maybe gotten a neighbor man to help him take the door off the hinges? He'd have got me inside in time for a second cup of coffee, to make the cookies, clean up some — Doris doesn't have the time for housekeeping I used to have — and do a sleeve at least of that sweater.

[Pulls handful of weeds.]

A good man, gone. Married late and widowed early. But we had our fifteen years, and he was a good, strong, loving man. When he retired, so did I. Happy, satisfying years.

[Closes eyes.]

Not romance as I taught my English literature students. Not romance as in the few movies we saw, where we shifted uneasily in our seats as silly actors kissed, their eyes going empty in a way to terrify you.

[Opens eyes.]

It was real... Jack never could get enough Chocolate Meringue Pie. Never. If he had one slice, he had two slices, and after some digesting, start over: one slice, two slices. I could have made that man so fat —

[Laughs.]

Pure inspiration. Came to me looking at blossoms in the garden. Take your nine-inch baked pie shell. In the top of a double boiler combine one cup sugar, tablespoon of cornstarch, quarter teaspoon of salt. Cut up three squares of chocolate — the best unsweetened you can find — and add it. Cut up some walnuts fine, add them. Add a teaspoon of vanilla extract, and stir in a cup of cold milk. Keep stirring over boiling water until it all thickens up. Then cover it and beat slightly the yolks of two eggs. Add a little of the hot mixture to them, then stir it all into the double boiler, stir like crazy. Cool it, then pour it into your baked pie shell, and add the meringue.

For the meringue, take the whites of three eggs. Beat until stiff with a dash of salt, and gradually, very gradually, beat in six tablespoons of sugar, until it's smooth and glossy. Then frost your pie, being certain to seal the edge of the crust, to prevent distortion in the baking. Use free strokes — make it look like a storm at sea. Place it in a moderately hot oven — three hundred, twenty-five degrees is good — until the tips of the waves look singed and the troughs take on the slightest color. Then let it cool. When cool cut it into six to eight slices. Best allow two slices a person. At least. And it's delicious. Delicious.

[Weeps.]

Violet, high time you went back to work. Time someone got the benefit of what you can do, even if they throw you back on the scrap heap again when you turn sixty-five. The grandmotherly life will wait for you. Till then go home to the desert and teach. Show the Navajo how to baste a hem, crochet a glove, how to bake pies. Show them what you know. Be useful. Do it while you can.

[Wipes eyes. Car approaches, horn sounds jauntily.]

My land. Home already?

[BLACKOUT]

[END OF PLAY]

www.ingramcontent.com/pod-product-compliance
Lightning Source LLC
Chambersburg PA
CBHW052008070526
44584CB00016B/1669